Praise for MentorShift at Work

"Bachman is an accomplished author and mentor with a powerful message. While many are great writers, what sets her apart is the heart she has for people, and how that heart shows up on every page. She has invested her creativity into this book that will guide mentor and mentee, no matter their level in an organization, to a more forward-looking and winning relationship."
—K. Michael Henshaw, CEO, Strategic intent Associates
Fmr. President, Lockheed Martin Missiles and Space

"Finally, an excellent step-by-step how-to for something that is critical to the success of any individual and organization. Bachman takes mentoring to a whole new level by making it an adventure that any company would eagerly incorporate. *MentorShift at Work* is such a great complement to the other tools that Bachman offers. It's a fun mentorship in and of itself!"
—Scott Halford, CSP, CPAE
CEO, Complete Intelligence, LLC
Wall Street Journal Best Selling Author of *Activate Your Brain*

"Lori Bachman deconstructs mentoring myths and rebuilds so you can shape your future workforce. Her intelligent and down-to-earth style is a stunning reflection of her genuine passion for mentoring. This purposeful approach provides a process for both mentors and mentees that gives your company the inside track to engaging employees and transferring critical knowledge to a new generation of leaders."
—Dr. Carol W. Carlson, Ph.D., P.E.
Denver Business Journal 2015 Outstanding Woman in Business in Architecture,
Engineering and Construction

"Mentoring is a vital necessity in the U.S. if we are to help students in high-need schools stay in school and on track to graduate ready for college and career. Kudos to *MentorShift at Work* for being part of this effort."
—Vanecia B. Kerr, Managing Director, Marketing, Communications and
Development, City Year Denver

"With *MentorShift at Work* our developing leaders have an additional tool to strengthen and perpetuate mentoring relationships. The engaging stories give perspective. The pithy quotes prompt thinking. The practical techniques spark momentum. The entire project makes mentors and mentees cycle up to the next level of effectiveness."
—Gregory C. Carlson, Ph.D.
Director, MA in Leadership Program
Trinity Graduate School
Trinity International University

MentorShift At Work

A Step-by-Step Guide to Creating
a Dynamic Mentoring Culture Within Your
Team, Department, or Organization

A Supplement to

Mentor

Shift

LORI BACHMAN

MentorShift at Work

For information about this title or to order other books and/or electronic media, contact the publisher:

MentorWorks
Publishing

MentorWorks Publishing
9173 Princeton St., Highlands Ranch, CO 80130
www.LoriBachman.com

Library of Congress Control Number: 2015911998
ISBN: 978-0-9913452-2-9
Printed in the United States of America

Cover and Interior design by: Adina Cucicov

Publisher's Cataloging-In-Publication Data
(Prepared by The Donohue Group, Inc.)

Bachman, Lori.
 MentorShift at work : a step-by-step guide to creating a dynamic mentoring culture within your team, department, or organization : a supplement to MentorShift / Lori Bachman.

 pages : illustrations, charts ; cm

 ISBN: 978-0-9913452-2-9

 1. Mentoring in business--Handbooks, manuals, etc. 2. Employees--Coaching of--Handbooks, manuals, etc. 3. Organizational learning--Handbooks, manuals, etc. 4. Corporate culture--Handbooks, manuals, etc. 5. Leadership--Handbooks, manuals, etc. I. Supplement to (work) Bachman, Lori. MentorShift. II. Title. III. Title: Mentor Shift at work

HF5385 .B332 2016
658.3/124   2015911998

"When I approach a child, he inspires in me two sentiments—tenderness for what he is and respect for what he may become."

— Louis Pasteur, French chemist and microbiologist

I dedicate this book to my children,
my most beloved mentees and mentors, Annie and Andrew,
With tender love for who you are and unflagging respect
for the woman and man you are becoming.

Table of Contents

Acknowledgements

I love quotes. I use them in my *MentorShift* book and now in its companion, *MentorShift at Work*. When I want to drive home a point, I search for a compelling quote. When I can't find the precise right words myself, I often find them in the words of another. When I want to underscore a deep feeling or passion, I often tap on a quote like the shoulder of an old, reliable friend.

Thus, the best way I can think of to thank the people who have contributed to my path is to share a quote for each group of my faithful helpers. I extend gratitude to the following wise guides and mentors; research, writing, and language gurus; friends and family.

> *"So the writer who breeds more words than he needs,*
> *is making a chore for the reader who reads."*
>
> **Dr. Seuss**

My editor, Toni Robino—It was a pure delight to work with you as you patiently coached me, edited my work, and helped me with just the words I need. You made writing fun.

> *"When you have a creative mind it doesn't stop going."*
>
> **Alison Moyet**

My creative writing mentor and friend, Sam Horn, The Intrigue Expert®—I learn about the power of words and intriguing messaging each time we meet.

My assistants—It was my pleasure to experience the creativity of these people: Jason Clark, Whitney Smith, research; Adina Cucicov, cover design and layout; and Danielle Snell, illustrations.

"The greatest gift of life is friendship, and I have received it."

H.H. Humphrey

My encouraging friends—You read and re-read every draft and cheered me on each step of the way: Robert Dalal, Kukana Sharpe, Linda Brisnehan and Stacey Dimercurio.

"A happy family is but an earlier heaven."

George Bernard Shaw

My family—Who gives me a glimpse of that pure heaven each day other than my parents, Joan and Bob, and my children, Annie and Andrew? You are always there and make each moment worthwhile.

I offer this last quote for you and me and all who seek to mentor well.

"Getting the most out of life isn't about how much you keep for yourself but how much you pour into others."

David Stoddard

Foreword

Leadership expert John C. Maxwell said, "People who add value to others do so intentionally. I say that because to add value, leaders must give of themselves, and that rarely occurs by accident."

I agree with Mr. Maxwell.

Lori Bachman is one of those rare individuals who positively impacts everyone she meets. She does that through her integrity, character and commitment to add tangible value so every interaction is a win for all involved—on the page and in person.

Lori Bachman's intention to add value and generously give everything she's learned as a Fortune 500 executive about creating productive, positive, high-performance cultures is evident in her book *MentorShift at Work: A Step-by-Step Guide to Creating a Dynamic Mentoring Culture Within Your Team, Department, or Organization.*

She provides real-life insights and examples that illustrate how you and your co-workers can build mutually rewarding relationships that ensure knowledge transfer and that leverage your employees' accumulated expertise and experience.

How does she do this? Three words come to mind:

- Engage
- Equip
- Multiply

First, the interactive exercises in *MentorShift at Work* show how mentors and mentees can *engage in high-priority, relevant, profitable projects that produce improved bottom-line results* for themselves and their organization.

Second, the *MentorShift* process *equips readers with an easy-to-understand-and-apply process* so they know exactly how to clearly and proactively communicate their needs, goals, requests, recommendations, insights and advice so everyone feels informed, updated and prepared to take appropriate actions that produce progress.

Third, *MentorShift multiplies impact* by creating a "rising tide raising all boats" culture of trust where everyone feels connected, heard, appreciated, and that they're a valued member of the team because they're contributing what they know.

Albert Einstein said, "Try not to become a person of success, but rather try to become a person of value."

In this important book, Lori shows that value and success are not mutually exclusive. Indeed, becoming a person of value—through effective mentoring—is the surest path to your organization and employees' ongoing success.

Sam Horn
Author of *Got Your Attention?* and *POP!*

Introduction

Welcome to the *MentorShift* workbook!

Have you ever been welcomed to a workbook? It sounds funny because I'm guessing you have never thought that a workbook could be anything but a "check the box and fill in the blank" exercise you did because you were required to do so. I have a teaching colleague who describes such an experience in that, after crafting an excellent workbook tool for her classes to use, she would witness her students scrambling to a far corner of the hall just minutes before class time to quickly scribble in a few answers in the workbook so they'd be "prepared" for the class. (Whew, they could check that box!) After all, it was a "work-book" and neither of those individual words necessarily inspired the students to heights of enthusiasm and engagement.

Well, I do welcome you to this workbook and I'm so glad you are here. You're about to learn and engage in a unique mentoring system. Up until now, you might have been in a mentoring relationship that was a great experience for you, or maybe less than you'd hoped for. Perhaps you've had no involvement at all with mentoring.

Whatever you've experienced in your past, during time spent with the MentorShift process, you will experience a matchless way to mentor and be mentored.

You will find that mentoring is not about being stapled, glued, or hammered to your chairs under the florescent lights of your office. It's not about prescriptive meetings once a month where mentors and mentees chat at the conference table and then the mentee beats feet back to their cubicle until the next monthly meeting.

You will put the four-step MentorShift process to use in a practical, hands-on way that will begin to deliver immediate results. What else will you gain from it?

The four-step MentorShift process is an ongoing process that educates, empowers, and equips you to pass the mentoring torch forward.

You will be a fully prepared mentor or mentee with a process under your belt that you can employ for the rest of your life. You might even have some fun, too. (Research shows that we learn best when we are a bit more relaxed and receptive.)

Here's an example of just that. When I worked in a corporate office setting, each employee was required to participate in an annual ethics training session. Now, I believe that businesses and individuals will fail themselves and their stakeholders if they don't diligently practice strong, robust ethical behaviors.

But, I'll be honest here: I often let myriad meetings overcome my making it down the hall to annual ethics training, knowing that I *would* make it, sooner or later, before the deadline. I would stall until either the last make-up session was ready to start or until my boss would stand, not amused, in my office doorway and say, "Bachman, you're on 'the list.' Hurry up and get to ethics training."

This occurred with an embarrassing degree of regularity, with the exception of two years. During those years, we had ethics training through the use of Dilbert videos, exercises, and cartoons. (Dilbert cartoons, created by Scott Adams, show the amusing daily foibles and frustrations of the micromanaged office worker, Dilbert, and his colleagues.) Over corporation-wide video presentation, our multi-billion dollar company CEO would introduce the Dilbert training, put his firm stamp of approval on the ethical principles as they were demonstrated in the Dilbert curriculum, and off we'd go.

We had fun! And I think it's telling that after all these years, those are the times I hurried to take part in the training, and still remember those ethics sessions.

For this reason, I decided that when I would write a book and a workbook to supplement it, especially about a topic like mentoring that has been overwrought, overworked, and underutilized, that I would do my utmost to make sure it was not "another boring business book." My goal for you is engagement and change, a SHIFT from the way its been done up until now. I've done my best to organize and infuse it with examples, exercises, practical tips, and even characters that will make the process enjoyable, and at the same time are founded on rock-solid learning principles. Follow these and they will make you a mentor or mentee that shines.

So let's get going with the MentorShift process in your mentoring relationship now.

Lori Bachman
Denver, Colorado

How to Use this Workbook

It's common in business books and workbooks today for the author to recommend, "You can read it straight through, or you can skim it, or you can dip in here and there from one chapter to another."

In the case of this *MentorShift* workbook, I will recommend otherwise. I highly recommend that you start at Module 1 and continue through to Module 9, reading and doing the exercises together with your mentor or mentee. Each module builds on the one before it; each process step stands on the work accomplished in the previous step.

If you already have found a mentor or mentee and have established a solid connection, you might want to move directly to Module 3, "Why is a Process Important?" and then return to Modules 1 and 2 for ideas on future mentoring relationships.

This workbook leads you through practical application of the theory and principles I laid out in the *MentorShift* book. It will deepen your understanding of the process and its underpinnings if you couple this workbook with the book itself. For those who use both together, I have notated throughout the workbook the applicable chapters in *MentorShift* where you can take a deeper dive into the material. At the same time, I intentionally created this workbook so that it could stand alone if you so choose.

Each module is organized in a similar format so you know what to expect.

- Body of knowledge and illustrations

- Preliminary questions to reflect upon

- The SHIFT Matrix

- The Planning Horizon (Modules 5 and 6)

- Summary and What's Next

Both mentor and mentee respond to the preliminary questions and populate the SHIFT matrix before getting together and then using it for discussion when they meet. That will make the most profitable use of your time.

If you'd like further learning about the elements of a module, I've included an Appendix section with additional resources and ideas for your reference. All sources are cited as endnotes in the end of the book. I also invite you to visit my website: **www.loribachman.com**.

My goal is to equip you with a mentoring process that you can use in your work life and, fortunately, the process transcends just that sphere. You can use it in your personal life and in any relationship you find yourself in that requires a prepared mentor and a willing and able mentee.

Resolve Your Mentor Tension

*How to Bust Through
Your Mentoring Roadblocks*

*"Often it isn't the mountains ahead that wear you out,
it's the little pebble in your shoe."*

Muhammad Ali, boxing legend

Remember the last time you had a pebble in your shoe? You were probably walking briskly along and suddenly all forward movement ground to a halt; you hopped on one foot and kicked your shoe to the concrete, then searched it for that pesky, painful obstruction. Not until you shook out the bothersome little piece of granite could you venture ahead on your path.

Reasons to avoid a mentoring relationship can be just like that pebble in your shoe. They can be small in size but feel large, and can stop all progress until they are found and removed. I call these mentoring impediments "The Seven Too Bs or Not Too Bs—Frequently Given Excuses to Avoid a Mentoring Relationship." What about you? Have you ever furtively sought a reason not to engage in a mentoring relationship your boss might have suggested?

Look through the list below and see if any of them strike a chord with you.

Too Busy (The last thing I need is one more thing to do.)

Too Boondoggled (Mentoring can't possibly do that much good; it's not value-added.)

Too Binding (I might enter a relationship that doesn't work for me, and ending it would be awkward.)

Too Bonding (My mentor/mentee might push the boundaries and make discussions uncomfortable.)

Too Baffling (I don't really know what I'm supposed to do in a mentoring relationship.)

Too Bottomed Out (I don't have the energy or motivation to take on something outside my comfort zone.)

Too Blocked (Even if I wanted to be a mentor or mentee, my management likely wouldn't support it.)

Any of these sound familiar to you? I have been the poster child at one time or another for all of them. Let's take a look back in time.

Five years into my career, my peer, Joe, encouraged me to start a mentoring relationship with a newbie who worked in our facility across town. The conversation went something like this: (parentheticals = my private thoughts)

- -

JOE: Hey Lori, why don't you consider mentoring Scott? He could learn something from you.

LORI: Me? Mentor? I don't think so. You have no idea what's on my plate. I'm up to my eyeballs in alligators. My boss just gave me the whole new business plan to finish by end of next quarter. (I'm very important and impressively busy, can't you see? —Too Busy)

JOE: That's almost six months from now! Can't you spare just a little time, maybe meet with him a couple times? He really needs someone to help him learn how to present a strong financial analysis to the boss.

LORI: C'mon Joe, I would, I mean I really think mentoring is great, at least sometimes, well, once in awhile. Honestly, it can be a waste of time. (Particularly a waste of MY time —Too

Boondoggled) Not only that, what if (he's a cling-on), um, he follows me around?—Too Bonding) and I can't get out of it if it's not working? (I need an escape hatch—Too Binding)

JOE: It's not like you're marrying him! Just meet with him a few times and give him some insights on how to present the analysis.

LORI: You know, I really would LOVE to (That's just a white lie, isn't it? Maybe that's not so bad?) but I know my boss, Rex, would put the brakes on it and block it from the start. (Thank Goodness!—Too Blocked) There's just too much work to be done. (And besides that I have no earthly idea how to mentor someone…So that, in and of itself, requires punting on this one.—Too Baffling) I wish I could help, but I just don't have the bandwidth right now (Should I feel guilty that I'd rather spend the time in my own office, which is, incidentally, right near the chocolate chip cookies and coffee in the vending machine? Nice.—Too Bottomed Out)

JOE: I know you don't want to do it but give it a little more thought. Or help me think of someone who might want to step up and give the guy a hand. (Did he have to end on that note?)

LORI: Okay, I'll see if someone comes to mind. (Whew! I'm off the hook.)

- -

The Seven Too Bs? I nailed them all! I had fervently and articulately defended that I could in no way mentor because I was:

1. Too Busy

    …and the mentoring process held the daunting threat of being…

2. Too Boondoggled

3. Too Binding

4. Too Bonding

5. Too Baffling

6. Too Bottomed Out

7. Too Blocked

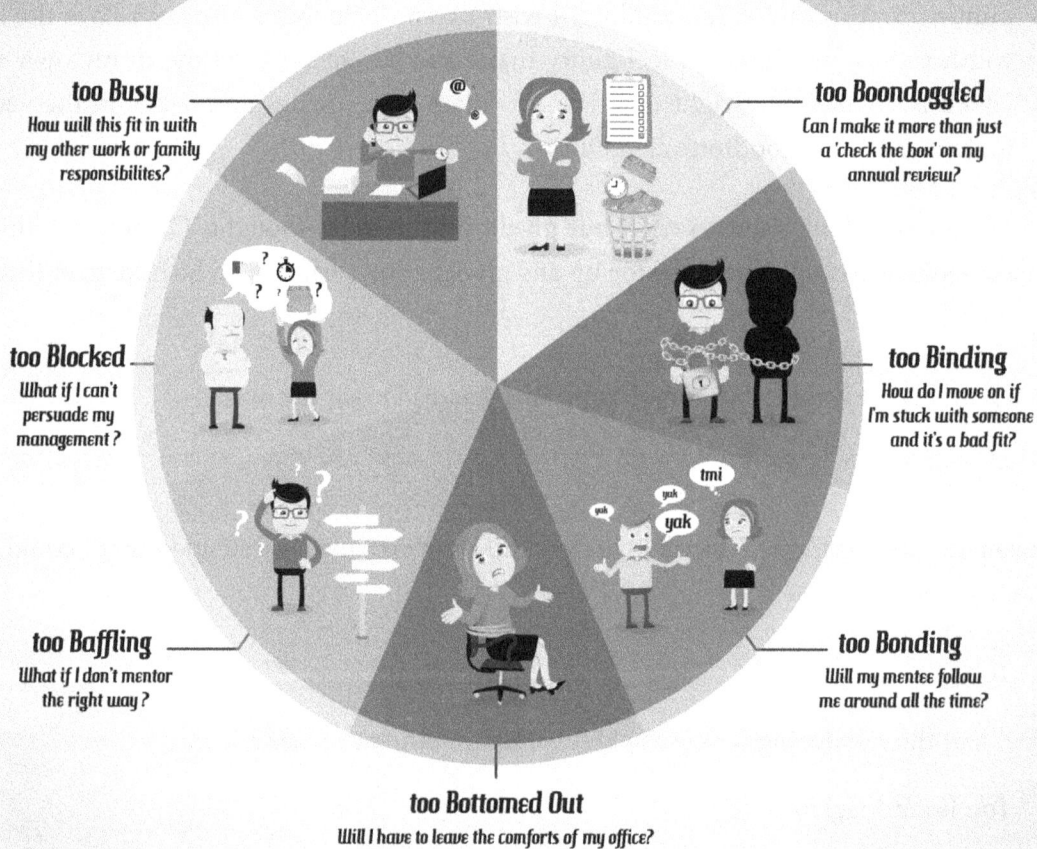

THE SEVEN TOO Bs OR NOT TOO Bs

FREQUENTLY GIVEN EXCUSES TO AVOID A MENTORING RELATIONSHIP

too Busy
How will this fit in with my other work or family responsibilites?

too Boondoggled
Can I make it more than just a 'check the box' on my annual review?

too Blocked
What if I can't persuade my management?

too Binding
How do I move on if I'm stuck with someone and it's a bad fit?

too Baffling
What if I don't mentor the right way?

too Bonding
Will my mentee follow me around all the time?

too Bottomed Out
Will I have to leave the comforts of my office?

TO FIND AN ANTIDOTE TO THESE EXCUSES, PICK YOURSELF UP A COPY OF
MENTORSHIFT AND CROSS THESE HURDLES WITH EASE.

www.loribachman.com

Whether you're about to become a mentor or a mentee, it's not unusual to have one or two of the Too Bs causing distress, duress, or the desire to stay close to your vending machine. Take heart! I overcame my abundance of reasons not to be in a mentoring relationship and I'm so glad I did.

I'm not saying that these Too Bs don't occasionally provide a legitimate reason not to be in a mentoring relationship. For instance, if you're truly too busy to mentor at a particular point in time, then opting out for that time is the right thing to do, both for you and your potential mentee. And if you're too busy to invest the time learning something new right now, then it wouldn't be fair to take up a potential mentor's time.

You might ask yourself, though, "How often do I hear myself saying, 'I'm too busy?" Is it an occasional necessary reason or a frequent habit?

Sometimes your management might put the stops on your mentoring due to project deadlines and commitments, and you must honor that. Hopefully this roadblock occurs only as the exception.

Let's take a moment for you to assess where you often find yourself in relation to the Too Bs.

Your Too Bs Assessment

Check the ones that are true for you.

_____Too Busy

_____Too Boondoggled

_____Too Binding

_____Too Bonding

_____Too Baffling

_____Too Bottomed Out

_____Too Blocked

It's good to look at what might make you hesitant about entering a mentoring relationship. You can address and resolve all of these Too Bs now that they have your attention and commitment.

How to Resolve Your Mentor and Mentee Tensions

I love stories about overcomers, don't you? These individuals have faced daunting challenges and in the end, climbed the mountain, crossed the finish line or witnessed an embryonic idea transform into a successful enterprise that bettered the lives of others. When I read or hear these stories, my current excuses for not being in a mentoring relationship diminish in size. The pebble doesn't seem like a boulder in my shoe; it's something I can kick out and move on.

Check out a few of these examples of overcomers[1]...

- Steven Spielberg, rejected from the University of Southern California, twice... Now one of most prolific filmmakers of all time (and current trustee of the university!).

- Albert Einstein didn't speak until he was four years old... He eventually developed the theory of relativity.

- Bill Gates' first company failed... He became founder of the giant, Microsoft.

- Richard Branson has dyslexia... but founded Virgin Airlines and is the fourth-richest man in the UK. Stephen King's first novel was rejected 30 times... Now he has sold 350 million copies worldwide.

- Erik Weihenmayer lost his vision at age 13... Then reached the summit of Mount Everest and the tallest peaks on each continent[2]

These are people with big stories and big outcomes. You can easily see that their results speak to the strength of their drive and determination. They pushed through their personal obstacles—through their version of their perceived Too Bs.

Not only mountain climbers and millionaires succeed because of their drive and determination; people in your own community set inspiring examples, as well. The manager of the nail salon near my home is one of those people. Quan is a soft-spoken, gentle man who fled Vietnam and sailed to Hong Kong to escape the repressive policies of post-war Vietnam.

Quan shared his story with me. At age 17, Quan, his elderly grandfather and younger brothers boarded a 23-foot boat with 15 other passengers to sail across the South China Sea. It was a perilous journey for all of them and a deadly journey for some. Quan bore the weight of caring for his grandfather and brothers and eventually brought them safely to the U.S. "I knew my goal and what I had to do," Quan said "I had to bring my family to safety. That was my only goal."

Quan knew what he had to do and he figured out how to do it. Not only did he take care of his family, he established a profitable business, got married, and had children of his own. He shares his experience with people who have moved to our community from different cultures. He mentors them in adjusting to all of the changes. He also understands the traumatic experiences many of them have had, so he can help them to find new meaning. He is walking proof that each day can be better than the one before.

Quan is a true overcomer. And what made him so effective? He had his goal clearly in mind.

Envisioning Your Goal Helps You Bust Through Your Roadblocks

Automaker and industrialist, Henry Ford, said, "Obstacles are those frightful things you see when you take your eyes off your goal."

By looking at the Too Bs, you've examined your obstacles to a mentoring relationship. Do you know what your goals are?

I believe that any and all of the Too Bs fade in importance once you identify WHY you really want to be a mentor or a mentee. Keeping that goal in front of you will help you bust through your Too Bs. When you lose sight of your goal, it's easy to stop trying.

One young woman's experience inspires us to realize the power of an envisioned goal.

In 1952, young Florence Chadwick stepped into the waters of the Pacific Ocean off Catalina Island, determined to swim to the shore of mainland California. She'd already been the first woman to swim the English Channel both ways. The weather was foggy and chilly; she could hardly see the boats accompanying her. Still, she swam for fifteen hours. When she begged to be taken out of the water along the way, her mother, in a boat alongside, told her she was close and that she could make it. Finally, physically and emotionally exhausted, she stopped swimming and was pulled out. It wasn't until she was on the boat that she discovered the shore was less than half a mile away. At a news conference the next day she said, "All I could see was the fog… I think if I could have seen the shore, I would have made it."

Two months later, Chadwick tried the crossing again, but this time was different. The same thick fog set in, but she made it because she said that *she kept a mental image of the shoreline in her mind while she swam*.[3]

11

Can you relate to the story of Florence Chadwick? Have you had a goal to mentor or be mentored but lost sight of why it was important to do it? Perhaps you've done it anyway because the boss said you needed to. Or maybe you've done it because it was part of your annual performance objective. Unfortunately these whys don't become whys that last.

Once you've driven a stake in the ground that marks "This is why I will mentor or be mentored," that goal will shine brighter than the fog created by the Too Bs.

Knowing the Why of Your Mentoring Relationship

Reflect for a moment on your mentoring goals. Why would you like to be in a mentoring relationship? Grab a pen and write two to three sentences that answer these two questions—"Why is mentoring an important and good thing to do?" and "Why do I personally want to be in a mentoring relationship?"

_____

_____

_____

_____

Was this easy to do? Sometimes figuring out the why behind the what and how takes some thinking.

Leadership expert, Simon Sinek, in his widely viewed TED talk, cites game changing companies and leaders with world-changing accomplishments—Apple, the Wright Brothers and Martin Luther King, Jr. Why did these leaders achieve the triumph that they did? Weren't there other equally capable competitors within their "market-space"?

Sinek purports that it is because these three leaders started with the why rather than the what or how of their mission. Below he describes the belief, the dream, the why of each leader.

Apple:

"Here's how Apple actually communicates. 'Everything we do, we _believe_ in challenging the status quo. We _believe_ in thinking differently. The way we challenge the status quo is by making our products beautifully designed, simple to use and user friendly. We just happen to make great computers. Want to buy one?'"

The Wright Brothers:

"Orville and Wilbur Wright had none of what we consider to be the recipe for success. They had no money; they paid for their dream with the proceeds from their bicycle shop; not a single person on the Wright brothers' team had a college education, not even Orville or Wilbur...the difference was, Orville and Wilbur were driven by a cause, by a purpose, by a belief. They *believed* that if they figured out this flying machine, it'd change the course of the world."

Martin Luther King, Jr.:

"Dr. King wasn't the only man in America who was a great orator. He wasn't the only man in America who suffered in a pre-civil rights America. In fact, some of his ideas were bad. But he had a gift. He didn't go around telling people what needed to change in America. He went around and told people what he believed. "*I believe, I believe, I believe,*" he told people. And people who believed what he believed took his cause, and they made it their own, and they told people."

Sinek continues, "... Inspired leaders and the inspired organizations—regardless of their size, regardless of their industry—all think, act and communicate *from the inside out.*"[4]

> Knowing why you believe mentoring is important and why you will engage in a mentoring relationship is the key to overcoming your obstacles.

Do your whys look anything like these?

- I want to mentor because I want to share essential knowledge, not keep it for myself.

- I want to mentor because I want to develop another person's gifts, not focus only on my own.

- I want to mentor because I can help someone learn to mentor another, and not let the value just stop with me.

- I want to be mentored because I believe it is one of the best ways to develop and grow.

- I want to be mentored so that I can learn first-hand from knowledgeable colleagues.

- I want to be mentored because I want to learn how to become an effective mentor myself and keep the cycle going.

These are some examples; you will have your own goals and whys. The important thing is to crystallize them so they're well defined.

Go back and reflect on what you've just written above. Does your goal say what you want it to? You will have time over the course of the four-step process to further cement the important "why" for yourself.

Author Benny Lewis said, "The difference between a stumbling block and a stepping stone is how high you raise your foot." You can kick those Too Bs pebbles out of your proverbial shoe and raise your foot high enough to overcome your stumbling blocks.

Using the SHIFT Matrix

Each module includes a SHIFT Matrix to be used as a talking tool between mentor and mentee. Here are a few guidelines for its best use:

- Mentor and mentee fill out their column ahead of their meetings

- Write as much or as little as you like

- Should take about 5-10 minutes to complete

- Meant to be a talking tool during your meet-up

- Each module shows an example and then includes a blank matrix for your use

MODULE 1	SHIFT MATRIX Resolve to Overcome Your Mentor Tension	
	Mentor	Mentee
S Share • What are my top Too Bs that have kept me from engaging in a mentoring relationship?		
H How • How are these Too Bs negatively affecting my life and/or career?		
I Insight • How might I benefit personally and professionally if I take the steps to change this?		
F Focus in • What can I do to change this? How will I bust through my Too Bs?		
T Task/Time • What will my next step be? When is my goal date for making this positive change?		

↑   ↑

Mentor   **Mentee**

Look back to the Too Bs you checked that apply to you and walk through the SHIFT you can make by resolving to overcome your obstacles.

MODULE 1	**SHIFT MATRIX (Example)** Resolve to Overcome Your Mentor Tension	
	(Mentor fills out this column)	(Mentee fills out this column)
S Share • What are the top Too Bs that have kept me from engaging in a mentoring relationship?	• *Too Busy*	• *Too Baffling* • *Too Binding*
H How • How are these Too Bs negatively affecting my life and/or career?	• *Not enough time with my family* • *Keeping me from developing a mentee* • *Stopping me from traveling recreationally*	• *Not knowing how to do something stops me from trying new things* • *I'm worried that a mentor might do more harm than good and that I won't know how to end the mentorship without causing hard feelings*
I Insight • How might I benefit personally and professionally if I take the steps to change this?	• *Expand my knowledge base to others at work* • *Make husband and kids happy* • *Make time to take a family vacation*	• *I could make a good connection with someone outside of my department* • *I could learn something new with expert guidance*
F Focus in • What can I do to change this? How will I bust through my Too Bs?	• *Delegate bi-weekly procurement meetings to my direct report to free up time* • *Goal to leave office NLT 6:00 p.m. each day*	• *Too Baffling—start mentoring relationship and go through MentorShift process* • *Share my concerns with potential mentors up front*
T Task/Time • What will my next step be? When is my goal date for making this positive change?	• *Let direct report know he will be taking over meeting—8/22* • *Start leaving office at 6:00 p.m.—8/25*	• *Start MentorShift process—9/1* • *Set up meeting with mentor and manager—9/6*

MODULE 1	SHIFT MATRIX Resolve to Overcome Your Mentor Tension	
	Mentor	**Mentee**
S Share • What are the top Too Bs that have kept me from engaging in a mentoring relationship?		
H How • How are these Too Bs negatively affecting my life and/or career?		
I Insight • How might I benefit personally and professionally if I take the steps to change this?		
F Focus in • What can I do to change this? How will I bust through my Too Bs?		
T Task/Time • What will my next step be? When is my goal date for making this positive change?		

Summary and What's Next

Knowing the "why" behind a mentoring relationship provides the solid and necessary foundation **to resolve your mentoring tension and obstacles**. In so doing, you can begin the four-step MentorShift process that will empower you to effectively equip others for success.

In Module 2, you'll learn more about how to find a mentor or mentee that's a good match for you.

Finding the Right Mentor or Mentee for You

Who and Where Are They?

"Show me a successful individual and I'll show you someone who had real positive influences in his or her life. I don't care what you do for a living—if you do it well I'm sure there was someone cheering you on or showing the way. A mentor."

Denzel Washington, actor

When Denzel Washington enrolled in Fordham University's drama program, he had no idea that his English teacher would play a leading role in his success. In addition to teaching English, Bob Stone was active in Fordham's theater program and had performed in successful Broadway shows. When Denzel told Bob he was passionate about becoming an actor, he encouraged him. "More than that," Denzel said "He believed in me."

After seeing Denzel perform in a student production of *Othello*, Bob wrote a glowing letter of recommendation for him for graduate schools. Denzel said, "What he basically said was, 'If you don't have the talent to nurture this young man, then don't accept him.'

"I must've read that letter a hundred times. Each time I thought, *Wow! If he thinks I'm that good then I'm going to have to live up to those words.* He put a fire under me. For years I kept that letter in my pocket—still have it. Whenever things became tough, I read it. There were times I wondered if I'd ever catch my first break, but Bob's words kept me going."

Through his university classroom, Denzel Washington found an impactful mentor in his professor, Bob Stone. Mr. Stone was clearly the "right mentor" for Denzel Washington at that point in his life and career—he engaged, encouraged him and promoted him to others. Many years later, after numerous awards and tributes in the acting profession, Denzel Washington still harkens back to those powerful words of his early mentor.[1]

How to Find the Right Mentor or Mentee for You— The Who and the Where

Finding a good mentor or mentee makes all the difference!

I've had ones that were, well, not so great (I'm speaking generously) and I've had ones that fantastically changed my life for the good.

I've had mentors who were parents (my own), a track coach, a pastor, a fellow author, an IT executive and an astronaut. I've had mentees that were children (mine), students, mothers, business executives, and new college hires.

I've found a mentor through "happenstance" and I've been matched with a mentee by an all-seeing, all-knowing mentor-matching application.

I've been referred to a mentor by a friend and requested as a mentor by a friend's friend. I met one at a citywide networking event, one on an airplane trip, had one "assigned" to me, and met another in the ladies room at work.

There are *many* "whos" and *many* "wheres" when it comes to choosing and connecting with your mentor or mentee, and some are more conventional than others.

In this module, you'll examine:

- Who is the type of person that would be a good mentor/mentee for you

- Where and how to find a good mentor/mentee for you

- How to conduct a successful MentorView

Let's start with a look at your mentoring experience to date. Think of the mentors you've had in your life. Take a moment and list them.

A. Note what character quality, talent, or skill drew you to them.

B. Note where you met them and how you connected with them.

I realize that individual lists will vary; some have had numerous mentors throughout their lives, others possibly just one. They might be formal (e.g., through a mentoring program) or informal mentors (e.g. parents, teachers, coaches, friends).

Next list the mentees you have had. Some of you might not have had a mentee yet; that is fine, it will happen soon. If you have mentored someone, list who and how you connected. In these relationships, you might not even have called yourselves mentor and mentee, but the relationship spurred you forward in growth and learning.

Your mentors/what drew you to them/how you met and connected:

1. _____

_____

2. _____

_____

3. _____

_____

Your mentees/what drew you to them/how you met and connected:

1. _____

   _____

2. _____

   _____

3. _____

   _____

You've heard the saying, "Variety is not the spice of life. It is the very stuff of it." Nowhere can you see that more clearly than the many ways individuals find their mentors/mentees. As you can see from your lists, these individuals have positively impacted you in some shape or form and there is no one "right way" to connect with a mentor or mentee.

WHO is Your Mentor Match? What Makes a Good Match?

You might be this far along in the MentorShift process and already have your mentor or mentee selected and settled. This module applies to you in that it guides you through a way of thinking about what you will look for in future relationships.

If you are at this spot and have not yet identified your mentor or mentee, by Module 4 you will need to have selected someone, so the timing is excellent and let's get down to the business of making a good selection for you.

Let's focus first in helping you identify your "WHO." What is that person like?

Research informs us as to what typically creates a good or bad mentor match. When focusing on the WHO, you'll likely find that these mentor match characteristics resonate with your values and preferences.

Check any that particularly strike you in terms of positive importance or negative impact:

What Makes a Good Mentor Match?	What Makes a Bad Mentor Match?
❏ Mentor and mentee share similar work ethics, career interests and educational background.[2]	❏ There is little to no trust between mentor and mentee.[7]
❏ Mentor and mentee have compatible hours, similar expectations of the relationship and shared goals and objectives.[3]	❏ Not setting, whether formally or through spoken word, an agreed-to "contract" (the goals, means, roles, plan of action, and timeline of relationship)[8]
❏ Mentor and mentee have similar cognitive styles; they think and problem solve in relatable ways.[4]	❏ Inability to see and measure change as a result of mentoring whether that be personal or company-wide[9]
❏ Mentee admires the mentor[5]	❏ Mentor cheering on the mentee without also giving constructive criticism. This falls short because the mentee doesn't grow and develop.[10]
❏ Mentee is open and receptive to the relationship and the information being shared.[6]	
❏ Mentor is willing to help mentee achieve his/her goal/s in the mentoring relationship.	❏ Mentor mistakes their own past successes as definite relevant advice to the mentee.[11]
	❏ Mentor talks all about themselves, without leaving room for questions from the mentee.
	❏ Mentee not being open and receptive to the knowledge and experience the mentor is sharing[12]

WHO is Your Mentor Match? Know your Preferences

Before you begin looking for potential mentors or mentees, take a minute to assess your preferences.

I want to find a mentor/mentee with these characteristics:

Department	**Rank/Position**
_____Inside	_____Above or below me in grade
_____Outside	_____Near peer
_____No preference	_____No preference

Company	**Gender**
_____Inside	_____Same
_____Outside	_____Different
_____No preference	_____No preference

Location	**Skill Set**
_____Local	_____Specific
_____Virtual	_____General
_____No preference	_____No preference

Experience	**Season of Life**
_____In my field/discipline	_____Ahead of me
_____Outside my field/discipline	_____Behind me
_____No preference	_____No preference

Mentees, as you progress into Module 4, Step 1: KNOW, you will take a deeper look into The Five Powerful Proficiencies™ that a mentor has to offer. For now, below you'll find a brief description of these proficiencies to help you kick-start your thinking about those talents and aptitudes that mean most to you in a mentor.

The Five Powerful Proficiencies™ in a Mentor

1. Pragmatics

You have specific skills that include practical how-to expertise, such as building a cohesive team, writing software code, analyzing a financial document or delivering a great presentation.

2. Passport

You can strengthen your mentee's network by introducing them to people that can help them reach their goals. Every mentor can benefit a mentee by offering introductions and some of you will be especially gifted passporters.

3. Presence

You command a presence, just by being in the room, and can offer an impressive example of how to handle authority and opposition.

4. Position

You hold a position that the mentee aspires to or wants to learn more about. If you mentor because of your position, you will reveal your real job description played out in real life.

5. Passion

You are passionate about your work and demonstrate how that inner fire supports your success.

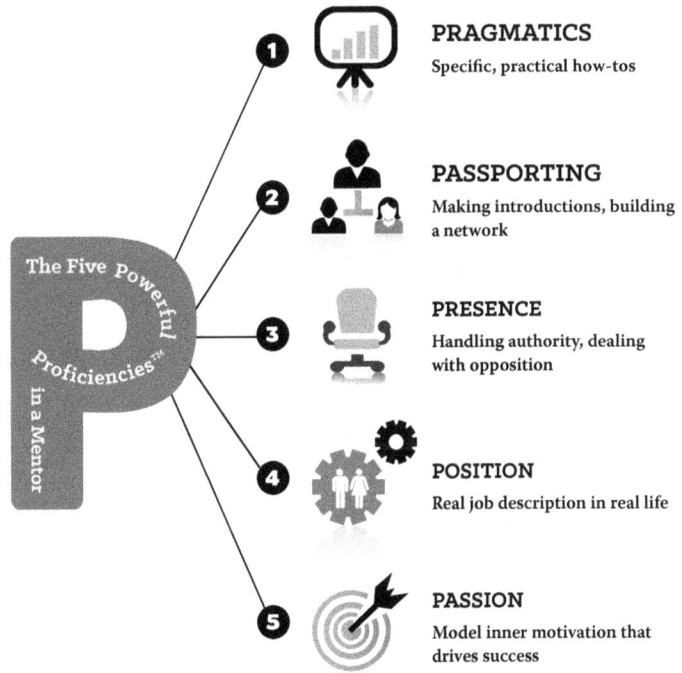

PRAGMATICS
Specific, practical how-tos

PASSPORTING
Making introductions, building a network

PRESENCE
Handling authority, dealing with opposition

POSITION
Real job description in real life

PASSION
Model inner motivation that drives success

Mentees, which of these proficiencies strike a chord in terms of what you would be looking for in a mentor? One or two? All of them?

Mentor, which of these describe where you are strong and where your strengths could benefit a mentee? Below, note which apply and why they hold importance to you.

_____

_____

_____

_____

WHERE is Your Mentor Match?

Now that you've reflected on what is important for you in a mentor, where might you find yours? Do you feel like it's looking for a needle in a haystack as you sort through an endless volume of resumes on LinkedIn? Or perhaps you hope you'll walk into your favorite coffee shop one morning and presto, just as you are ordering your grande latte with chocolate caramel drizzle, the leader you'd been wishing for stands right behind you in line. Or maybe you'll meet at your workplace or perhaps at your leadership meet-up group.

Here are some places that well-known mentors and mentees have connected:

Swimmer Michael Phelps met his mentor Bob Bowman while training at the North Baltimore Aquatic Club. Bowman immediately saw Michael's potential and competitive drive and became his coach.[13] (Through a common interest/passion.)

Charles Schwab started as a messenger at Carnegie Steel in the late 19th century, when he endeared himself to the tycoon with his enchanting piano playing at a party. Carnegie appointed a 35-year-old Schwab as his successor in 1897. Schwab would later run Bethlehem Steel, the second-largest steel company in the world.[14] (Through happenstance.)

Oprah Winfrey credits her fourth-grade teacher for much of her success. "[Mrs. Duncan] often stayed after school to work with me," she said, "helping me choose books and letting me grade her papers."[15] (Through a learning environment.)

As the Facebook chief operating officer's economics professor and thesis adviser at Harvard, Larry Summers helped Sheryl Sandberg land jobs at the World Bank and the U.S. Department of the Treasury.[16] (Through a work setting.)

Whether you meet on a social media site, at your work or school, or through a chance encounter, being proactive about creating your plan to meet your potential mentor or mentee will open up many possibilities.

WHERE is Your Mentor Match—It's Not Just a Cookie Cutter Situation

Recently I held a focus group of mid- to senior-level executives. They had collectively read my book, *MentorShift,* and we were discussing specific topics of interest to them. Although we covered the gamut that evening, the participants returned repeatedly to this topic of finding the right mentor. They asked, "How do I find a mentor if I..."

- Live in a different city? (virtual)

- Am between jobs?

- Want someone outside of my direct reporting line?

- Want someone outside my own company?

- Work remotely?

- Work in a company that doesn't have a mentoring program?

- Am looking for a peer mentoring relationship?

- Want only an informal relationship?

Many of these scenarios spoke directly to the question of locating a desirable mentor when work or personal circumstances posed a challenge, a "non-cookie-cutter" situation. In circumstances such as these, the **power of networking** is the key. Geography, job positioning, in-between assignments and the rest can all be effectively addressed with mentees proactively reaching out to their networks and their "networks' networks." To that end, begin to address who those network touch points would be for you.

List three people in your immediate network that can help you to find a mentor or mentee.

1. _____

2. _____

3. _____

List three colleagues who have had a successful mentoring relationship, and would recommend their mentor/mentee as a potential for you.

1. _____

2. _____

3. _____

List the name of the organizations or clubs you belong to or are familiar with that might have a mentor or mentee for you in their membership.

1. _____

2. _____

3. _____

If you could ask anyone you know, either who you know well or from afar, to be a mentor/mentee, who would that person be? When you identify that person, who is someone in your network that has a connection with them?

1. _____

2. _____

3. _____

Finding a mentor or mentee is a calculated risk, and you need to be willing to lean forward to make it happen. You might not find exactly what you were hoping for in each mentoring connection, but chances are that after conducting a MentorView, you will multiply your chances of success.

Mentor + Interview = MentorView—Be Prepared, Be Clear!

Mentee, to kick things off, you will need to do "The Big Ask." That's simply a matter of requesting a brief meeting time with a potential mentor (which I refer to as the MentorView) with the goal of seeking further help in a specific area (Chapter 18 and 19, *MentorShift*). If the potential mentor agrees to meet with you, your goal is to optimize that time together so you know if there's enough common ground to make a good mentoring match. There are some important ways to prepare prior to the MentorView.

Jamie, a new college hire, had asked for some of my time to investigate a possible mentoring relationship. I agreed to meet with her for a half hour to explore it. I'd heard good feedback about her work ethic and attitudes, and was at a place where I could take on another mentee.

When we held our discussion, she came in prepared and impressed me with what she had taken the time to find out. She asked questions and knew my background and the kinds of assignments I'd had. She had studied my career trajectory and had learned about my current project. It was clear she had taken the time to prepare.

She made such a great impression! You can do the same by taking a little time before you meet with a potential mentor for the first time.

Mentee, before your scheduled MentorView:

1. Learn these things about your potential mentor:

    ○   Areas of expertise

    ○   Educational background

    ○   Awards and certifications

    ○   Common interests

    ○   Recent successes

2. Check out these resources:

    ○   LinkedIn—essentially a snapshot of their resume

    ○   Any company Interweb tools you may have

    ○   Google search for their personal sites/blogs

    ○   Google Scholar to see if they have been published or mentioned in any academic research

    ○   If you were connected by a friend/acquaintance/HR department, ask them for background information

3. Write a sentence or two explaining what you'd most like to learn from your potential mentor. Be CLEAR on what you are hoping to accomplish so you can communicate that to them.

4. Clean up your online presence. (That college photo of you wearing a toga and toasting the crowd might have to go!) You want to win points, not lose them.

5. Send your potential mentor your bio, CV or resume along with a concise email clearly stating why you would like to explore a mentoring relationship with them.

For our purposes, the Module 2 SHIFT Matrix will serve as a template for how a MentorView can and should flow. Mentee, you will populate your portion of the SHIFT Matrix prior to your meeting, and it's worth asking your potential mentor if they would be willing to do the same. (If you aren't comfortable yet with asking your potential mentor to fill out the SHIFT Matrix, do fill out the mentee side to better articulate your hopes for the relationship. You can take it with you to the MentorView to demonstrate that you are thinking proactively.) This matrix provides a discussion tool that can assist you in deciding whether the relationship will go forward.

MODULE 2	SHIFT MATRIX (Example) The MentorView	
	Mentor	**Mentee**
S **Share** • What do both mentor and mentee generally want from a relationship? Mentee, what are you specifically seeking to learn?	• *Share how my position works, who I have to interface with, how I deal with conflict* • *Help mentee position themself for success with their specific goals*	• *Learn more about how to set a long-range career plan for myself* • *Learn more about how to navigate office politics* • *Learn how to conduct effective meetings*
H **How** • How would you like a relationship to work? (e.g., frequency of meetings, duration, beginning/end, topic, content, etc.)	• *I'm free to meet once a month on a scheduled basis* • *I'm open to inviting a mentee with me to meetings and events to have some more time together*	• *I'd like to meet once a month* • *I'd like to attend some networking events with my mentor*
I **Insight** • What is it about this mentoring relationship possibility that appeals to you most?	• *Mentee has a good reputation for hard work and taking projects seriously* • *Mentee is currently working in same product line, so there is synergy for the area*	• *Potential mentor has had several of the jobs that I would like have at some point* • *I am working on how to deal with conflict effectively and I know my potential mentor is good at that*
F **Focus in** • If you go forward, are there any challenges or limitations the other person needs to know about?	• *Frequent travel, often unexpectedly, which could impact set meeting times*	• *I work from my San Diego office two weeks a month* • *I'm currently in a position that I'm trying to leave*
T **Task/Time** • When will you make a decision about going forward or not? If so, when and where will you convene next? What will you have prepared for next meeting?	• *Will decide within a week of this meeting*	• *I'd like to have the decision by next week. I'd like to continue forward with this if my potential mentor is up for it. I'd like to get together our first time by October 15*

MODULE 2	**SHIFT MATRIX** The MentorView	
	Mentor	**Mentee**
S Share • What do both mentor and mentee generally want from a relationship? Mentee, what are you specifically seeking to learn?		
H How • How would you like a relationship to work? (e.g., frequency of meetings, duration, beginning/end, topic, content, etc.)		
I Insight • What is it about this mentoring relationship possibility that appeals to you most?		
F Focus in • If you go forward, are there any challenges or limitations the other person needs to know about?		
T Task/Time • When will you make a decision about going forward or not? If so, when and where will you convene next? What will you have prepared for next meeting?		

After Your MentorView—Is It a Good Match?

Ask yourself these questions after meeting together. They will provide a debrief for you and help you decide if you plan to go forward. (Circle your answer)

1. Did you feel comfortable in the MentorView?

    Very   Somewhat   Marginal   Not at all

2. Was it easy for you to understand each other?

    Very   Somewhat   Marginal   Not at all

3. Do you have similar time and schedule demands?

    Very   Somewhat   Marginal   Not at all

4. What character traits does the mentor/mentee have that will benefit you—even if you don't particularly like those traits?

    _____

    _____

5. Did you learn anything in the MentorView to make it a deal breaker for you?

    _____

    _____

(If you decide to go forward after the MentorView, it's a good faith step for the mentee to set up the first get together.)

All Mentors and Mentees Have Something to Offer—Decide Which One Is for You!

Before we leave this module, I'll introduce you to some interesting characters. In my book *MentorShift*, I created a group of ForMentors and TorMentors (and now their alter egos, the ForMentees and TorMentees) to give you a glimpse into some common mentoring styles and characteristics to either pursue, adjust to, or in some cases totally avoid. Surely you've encountered bits and pieces of all of these along the way.

FORMENTORS: Generally individuals want to find (and be) AchieveMentors, CommitMentors, DevelopMentors, and EnjoyMentors. These mentors are effective in helping their mentees accomplish their goals in an enjoyable manner. (Chapters 20-24, *MentorShift*)

TORMENTORS: TorMentors can also be effective in helping their mentees accomplish their goals—the mentee just needs to exercise some finesse in navigating the mentor's idiosyncrasies. TorMentors are known as By-the-BookMentors, Drive-ByMentors, ArguMentors, and HoverMentors, but they're not really such bad guys, if you can harness the right techniques and attitudes when dealing with them. I've had ample input from satisfied mentees who learned to communicate well with a TorMentor and come out a winner. (Appendix A-7, *MentorShift*)

It's worthwhile to ask yourself, "What do I see of these Mentors/Mentees' characteristics in me?"

ForMentors are the mentors that we click with, have an easy time relating to, and really like. The same goes for ForMentees!

Adam AchieveMentor

Adam the AchieveMentor will make sure you get what you need and want out of the mentorship and set a great example for reaching goals.

The AchieveMentee will take on every assignment and task with enthusiasm and press for more.

Callie the CommitMentor is true blue every time—always there when you need her, she'll stick with you until you've done what you set out to do.

The CommitMentee will take the mentorship very seriously and rarely miss a meeting or a deadline.

Callie CommitMentor

<u>Dan the DevelopMentor</u> is a master of helping his mentee capitalize on their strengths and expand their visions for success.

The DevelopMentee will do everything possible to grow, expand and improve.

<u>Emma the EnjoyMentor</u> will somehow make everything she teaches fun and entertaining. She's passionate about enjoying life and work.

The EnjoyMentee is a breath of fresh air—very positive, friendly, and fun.

Dan DevelopMentor

TorMentors are the mentors you sometimes need, but wish you didn't. No matter what category you place a potential mentor in, if you respect them, admire their accomplishments, abilities, or talents, or they can help you turn a weakness into a strength, they're worth considering! And the same is true for TorMentees.

Emma EnjoyMentor

Let's say you're a rising star, but on your evaluations, you receive a consistent criticism that you're prone to making assumptions that bite you in the bottom line. Well, <u>Augie the ArguMentor</u> can help you to question your own assumptions and perform the necessary due diligence before you take a stance.

The ArguMentee will ask questions that you've never thought about and may help you build a stronger case or learn something that expands your awareness or shifts your perspective.

If your manager keeps telling you that you need to strengthen your attention to details, there are lots of things you can learn from <u>Betty By-the-BookMentor</u>.

Augie ArguMentor

The By-the-BookMentee will be a stickler about following the Mentor-Shift process, which can make the mentoring relationship easier or more straightforward for the mentor. Mentors might also gain a new appreciation for the consistency of following a process.

Betty By-the-Book-Mentor

Harry HoverMentor

If you're having a hard time meeting your deadlines and staying accountable to yourself, a few weeks with <u>Harry HoverMentor</u> can help you to develop better habits.

The HoverMentee can become your "go to" guy or gal or be the shadow you can't shake, depending on how you lead them. Carry a prioritized list of tasks so you can give the HoverMentee meaningful assignments whenever they appear at your side.

Even <u>Dayna the Drive-ByMentor</u> can be an asset if she has the expertise to weigh in on your special project from time to time and you're not looking for a more formal mentoring schedule.

The Drive-ByMentee is usually juggling a lot of projects and may only have time for a quick check-in visit from time to time. This would be frustrating for a By-the-BookMentor but it can be a time-saver for other mentors.

(As you continue through the MentorShift workbook. you'll see these ForMentors and TorMentors pop up here and there to brighten the way.)

Dayna Drive-ByMentor

Summary and What's Next

There are many ways and means to connect with a mentor or mentee that is right for you. The best chance of success occurs when the mentee is clear on what they are looking for and proactive in their search.

In Module 3, you will examine why a process is important and how it underscores the way you learn and transfer knowledge most effectively.

Why Is a Process Important?

A Reliable Process Makes All the Difference

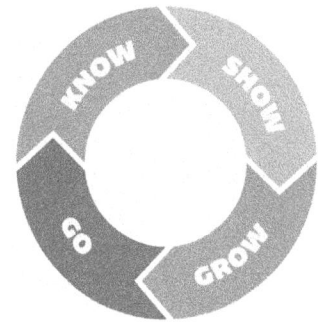

Excellence is a continuous process and not an accident.

Dr. Abdul Kalam, political leader

It was a picture-perfect day to begin a fishing expedition in outer space. All conditions were optimal as NASA was preparing to send a new satellite into orbit. The Atlantis space shuttle bay held an enormous reel of "fishing line" that was connected to the satellite. The plan for the Tethered Satellite Mission (TSS) was to unwind the reel until the satellite reached its appointed distance, 12 miles away. Dragging the satellite would generate electricity along the tether as the shuttle and the satellite raced through Earth's magnetic field at 17,500 miles per hour.

NASA and its satellite team had labored over this project for two decades. Fantastic science would be gathered from this mission that would pave the way to eventually erect space stations, string extensive radio antennas and generate electricity for operating spacecraft. But it didn't turn out to be a perfect day for fishing after all. The copper and fiber cable unwound only 840 feet before jerking to a stop. The "fishing reel" had jammed.[1]

A bolt, only a quarter of an inch in diameter, had snagged the tether and prevented it from moving all the way to its 12-mile stopping point. The fallout? More than $376 million was spent to no avail. NASA didn't capture the game-changing research and jobs were ultimately lost. Thanks to a quarter-inch bolt.

Of course, NASA couldn't place blame on a tiny piece of steel. The investigation pointed to a design and testing process that had come up short and failed to foresee the finite measurements and subsequent physics of the unwinding reel and its hardware. After the mission failure, engineers worked double time to understand how the process had failed and how it could be rectified for further missions. They needed to be able to rely on their process.

What's so Great About Processes?

A reliable process breeds trust, propels progress and brings satisfaction to its users. When a process designer creates a good process, then communicates and implements it effectively, what is the result? It enables the user to rely on the process. We all depend on hundreds, if not thousands, of processes every day.

To name just a few:

- An automobile that arrives safely at its destination
- A smartphone that alerts its owner as to their daily appointments
- An IT system that delivers timely data to its users
- An ER team that saves people's lives

The Power of Process

The power of an effective process cannot be underestimated. Just ask Jack Welch, former Chairman and CEO of General Electric. In 1995, he selected GE's "best and brightest" to learn the process improvement system called Six Sigma and put those methods into action. And it worked. Welch later wrote that the Six Sigma process helped drive operating margins to 18.9 percent in 2000 from 14.8 percent four years earlier[2] and provided estimated benefits on the order of $10 billion during the first five years of implementation.[3]

Betty By-the-Book-
Mentor

"Processes you say? I have processes to develop processes. And I have them all catalogued meticulously so I don't make one false step!"

The formal program dubbed Six Sigma looks for waste—for defects in processes, like the unsuccessful test procedure that would have identified the errant TSS bolt. It then rids the process of those stumbling blocks, thereby reducing costs and hefting up revenue.

Welch and his commitment to process improvement was just the beginning. An entire industry has grown around process analysis and improvement. Thousands of companies have poured millions of dollars into the Six Sigma disciplined, data-driven approach for eliminating defects in any process—from manufacturing to transactional and from product to service.[4]

Good processes benefit everyone, and those dedicated to good processes reap rewards. Let's consider Six Sigma again for a moment. It takes a lot for a worker to attain a Six Sigma certification through many hours of coursework and conducting process analysis. But it pays off. An individual who holds a Six Sigma Certification can earn anywhere from 5 to 15 percent more money based on their level of knowledge, experience, and expertise.[5]

According to the Six Sigma Academy, Black Belts (a high level of Six Sigma competency) save companies approximately $230,000 per project and can complete four to six projects per year. (Given that the average Black Belt salary is $80,000 in the United States, that is a fantastic return on investment.)[6]

> Not everyone can or will employ a rigorous approach such as the Six Sigma program, but *all businesses value reliable processes and workers who can train others in those processes.*

Is Your Current Mentoring Process Reliable?

What about a mentoring process? What's it like in your company? Is there even a process in place? Let's leave the rigors of Six Sigma measurement and just observe how it plays out in your workplace. I have some guesses and I would put good money on them.

- You have a formal mentoring program. Mentor and mentee meet at an appointed time in the office, discuss the issue *du jour*, then the mentee leaves and likely returns the next month for more of the same.

- You have no mentoring program *per se* but you wish you had a mentor. You might check with Antoine down the hall or Maria in the next cubicle to see if they might be up for helping you out. You'll ask them tomorrow. If they say yes, you will meet next week to talk about your career. That will be your mentoring process.

These two models sum up the majority of mentoring you will likely observe. I recently asked a senior executive in a multi-million-dollar consulting firm about how well their mentoring process was working, and he said, "Mentoring process? Now that's a good concept. We ought to look into that."

I'll bet you'll agree. We've got a ways to go.

The MentorShift Process to the Rescue

The MentorShift process removes the questions so mentors never have to feel that mentoring is Too Baffling, Too Boondoggled, or any of the other Too Bs. Mentees can relax, knowing they will learn efficiently and comfortably.

MentorShift employs the best practices of effective knowledge transfer—observation, learning by doing, and independent action.

A top-level view of the MentorShift process is as follows: (Throughout the process, "I" refers to the mentor and "You" to the mentee for ease of identification and consistency.)

Step 1—KNOW (I Do)

Mentors must **know** their subject matter well as they share knowledge; they **know** the skills and talents they confidently possess to best benefit their mentees.

Step 2—SHOW (I Do, You Contribute)

Mentors **show** their mentees the skill/talent/task as the mentee observes; mentee contributes to the task to strengthen learning.

Emma EnjoyMentor

"C'mon, Betty, lighten up! Kick back a bit and if you mess up the process the first time, just shake it off and do it again!"

Step 3—GROW (You Do, I Contribute)

Mentees **grow** as they move forward into the leadership role; mentor contributes by offering encouragement and support.

Step 4—GO (You Do)

Mentees have become fully independent and equipped to **go** perform the task; mentors **go** on to mentor again.

At the end of this workbook you will have acquired a proven mentoring process that you can transfer to others.

MODULE 3	SHIFT MATRIX (Example) Why Is Process Important?	
	Mentor	**Mentee**
S Share • What have I learned to do by following steps in a process?	• *Play tennis* • *Build a piece of furniture by following the directions* • *Set up a new website*	• *Ballroom dance class my spouse and I took* • *Program software code and test it*
H How • How have I seen a step process work effectively? Ineffectively?	• *Effectively—with building the website, following the process made it come together efficiently* • *Ineffectively—I've seen groups adhere so closely to following a process by the book that it becomes boring and hurts creativity*	• *Effectively—I learned to program code correctly; when something didn't go right I would go back to the previous step* • *Ineffectively—Sometimes the code writing steps weren't exactly right so I would spend a lot of time correcting them*
I Insight • How could following a mentoring process improve the quality of mentoring relationship outcomes?	• *It would be good because sometimes mentors and mentees don't know exactly what to do together* • *I'd be better able to measure how it is going*	• *I would know what I need to be doing as a mentee* • *I would have specific goals and a timeline*
F Focus in • What can I do to make a mentoring process effective?	• *Show up and be on time!* • *Be sure I'm consistent in getting together with my mentee so the process has a chance to work*	• *I can do any "homework" we have in between meeting up with one another* • *I can ask questions about the process when I don't understand it*
T Task/Time • What will my next step be? What is my goal date for making this positive change?	• *Start MentorShift process—9/1* • *Read the accompanying chapters in "MentorShift"*	• *Start MentorShift process—9/1* • *Read the accompanying chapters in "MentorShift"*

MODULE 3	SHIFT MATRIX Why Is Process Important?	
	Mentor	**Mentee**
S **Share** • What have I learned to do by following steps in a process?		
H **How** • How have I seen a step process work effectively? Ineffectively?		
I **Insight** • How could following a mentoring process improve the quality of mentoring relationship outcomes?		
F **Focus in** • What can I do to make a mentoring process effective?		
T **Task/Time** • What will my next step be? What is my goal date for making this positive change?		

45

Summary and What's Next

Reliable processes make learning and transferring skills more effective. You see it regularly in your business and everyday life. It's doubly important in an area such as mentoring, where processes tend to be lacking.

In Module 4, you'll take a look at the first step in the MentorShift process: KNOW, "I Do."

Step 1: KNOW
"I Do"

The Five Powerful Proficiencies

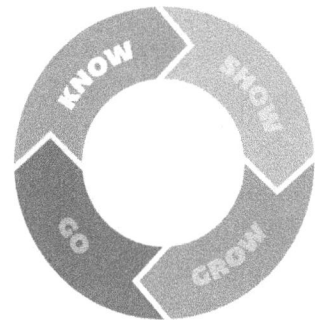

"Know yourself. Don't accept your dog's admiration as conclusive evidence that you are wonderful."

Ann Landers, columnist

Yes! My dog, Coco, indeed thinks I'm wonderful (dogs are so smart) and I'll happily agree with my little mutt's conclusion and thus take a different tact on Ms. Landers' advice. Maybe my dog knows something about me that I don't see as clearly. She is over the moon when she lays eyes on me, night or day, whether I've been gone two days or two minutes, because she sees her loving "non-fur person," a safe place, a friend, a master and provider of all things delectably crunchy to eat.

She recognizes my strengths and all that I have to offer her. Her wet, sloppy kisses put the punctuation mark on all that's good and strong about me.

As you'd imagine, though, my dog is not the final word; let's revisit Ms. Landers' quote, because there is deep insight in it. She begins with "Know yourself." I believe she means, "Take an honest look at what you have to offer, both the lovely and strong, the warts and all, and don't rely only on the outlook of admirers (be they canine or otherwise) around you."

Know yourself. For how can you best mentor someone if you are not in tune with the strengths and skills you possess?

I discovered this through my writing journey that began several years ago. Shereen El Seki, former correspondent for *The Economist*, said, "If you really want to know yourself, start by writing a book." I read that quote and thought, "Truer words were never spoken."

When I began to write *MentorShift*, I took my normal "leap in" approach to a new project. "Dive right in and kick this bad boy out in no time," I said to myself, "it will be fun!" By the end of the first year, reality had set in. What I thought I could complete in three weeks took three months; what I thought would require two rewrites took more than I care to count. And then there was social media and marketing. People began to ask me, "What is your marketing roll-out plan and distribution strategy?" They might as well have been speaking in Pig Latin. I'd hesitate and say, "Let me get back to you on that." I wanted to head for the hills.

Finishing a book is a profoundly rewarding experience. It also is a profound way to know yourself, both strengths and challenge areas, better than you've ever known them before. It's a deep dive into where you have fortitude, knowledge and motivation; it's a bright and constant light on what you really don't know.

I began to tally up my Strengths and Challenges.

Strengths—I can write easily, I'm a good storyteller, I understand grammar and sentence structure, and I can speak freely and joyfully about my book's ideas.

Challenges—I need help navigating all of the many avenues of social media, troubleshooting computer malfunctions, understanding the publishing industry and keeping track of all the book sales through online, book fairs, speaking engagements.

Yikes, where's Coco now?

How does this relate to mentoring? My strengths listed above are both general and specific, as are my challenges.

Specific Strengths	General Strengths
Write easily	Communication through written word
Storytelling	Creativity
Speaking about book ideas	Teaching through the spoken word

Challenges	
Social media/Computer	Technology
Publishing industry and marketing	Public relations and marketing
Keeping track of sales	Administration

Where do I most frequently mentor others?

In my areas of strength, of course! My mentees would be left wanting if I were to teach topics outside of my strength areas.

What about you? Have you taken a good look at where you're strong and where you can most effectively pass on life and career skills? (For a helpful list of sites for strength evaluations, refer to Appendix A)

This is the essential place to start. In Step 1, as a mentor you need to **KNOW** your subject matter and how best to share it. As a mentee, you need to **KNOW** what you are seeking to learn.

Mentee, in the following set of questions, we will walk through the Five Powerful Proficiencies™. We will begin with Pragmatics and shine a special spotlight on that proficiency because the "Pragmatics Project" that you and your mentor will determine together will be central throughout your mentoring time together and will yield you tangible results that you desire. It will keep your relationship directed and on target.

To hone in on your Pragmatics Project, take some time to reflect on these questions as you determine where you'd like to specifically focus:

Ask yourself:

- What am I working on, or

- What will I be working on, or

- What would I like to be working on?

49

Examples:

- Writing software code for a technical program

- Designing an engineering solution for our core line of business

- Building a component or sub-system on the factory line

- Developing a year-end financial report for senior management

- Presenting program status to our investors and customers

- Implementing a new compensation process for our benefits organization

When identifying your Pragmatics Project with your mentor, be certain to follow these elements:

- Project start and estimated finish

- Specifics on what you hope to accomplish

- Measurable result

I often share with my clients this thought, *"Mentoring is not only about relationships; it is also about results."* As you and your mentor identify and solidify your Pragmatics Project and work together on the desired results, your relationship naturally follows and strengthens.

At this point, brainstorm a couple of Pragmatics Projects in your current sphere that are relevant and meaningful to you.

\#1 _____

_____

\#2 _____

_____

There's more to come on your Pragmatics Project. Now we'll move on to the other four Powerful Proficiencies.

Powerful Proficiencies Self-Assessment

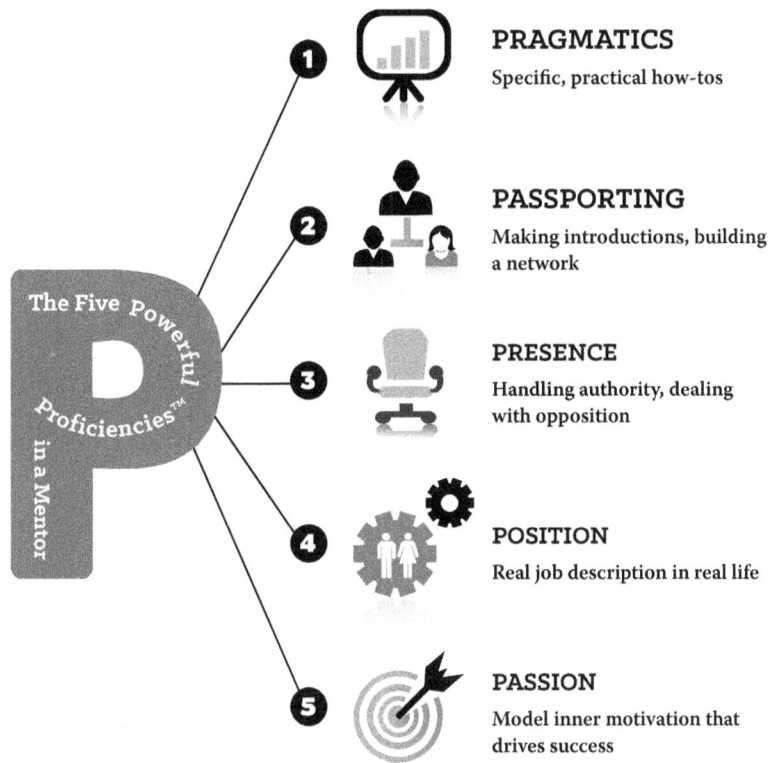

1 **PRAGMATICS**
Specific, practical how-tos

2 **PASSPORTING**
Making introductions, building
a network

3 **PRESENCE**
Handling authority, dealing
with opposition

4 **POSITION**
Real job description in real life

5 **PASSION**
Model inner motivation that
drives success

The Five Powerful Proficiencies™ in a Mentor

Mentor, list three skills or methods for each proficiency that you can share. Mentee, list three skills or methods that you would like to learn.

Pragmatics

Pragmatics includes specific crafts or skills with a beginning and end and often a completed product.

Mentors: What specific skills or practical how-to expertise can you teach?
Mentees: What specific skills or practical how-to expertise do you want to learn?

Examples:

- Write software code
- Design a complex engineering solution
- Build a component on a factory line
- Analyze a financial document

Passport

Making introductions and strengthening the mentee's network give a valuable component to many mentoring relationships.

Mentors: List three introductions you could make that would benefit your mentee.
Mentees: List three people in your mentor's network that you would like to meet.

1. _____

2. _____

3. _____

Presence

The somewhat intangible element of commanding a presence is best learned by observation and your brain's mirror neurons will facilitate that process.

Mentors: In what arena or arenas do you command presence? Is it giving a presentation in the boardroom, closing a deal on the phone, pitching a new idea on the golf course, or effective interactions at social events and networking functions?

Mentees: In what arenas would you most like to watch and learn how to increase your presence?

1. _____

2. _____

3. _____

Position

Sometimes a mentoring relationship is formed to teach and learn about a particular position.

Mentors: List your current position along with two other positions that you've held that your mentee might benefit by learning more about.

Mentees: List your current position along with two other positions that you aspire to achieve.

Current Position: _____

Mentor's Past Positions:
Mentee's Positions to Aspire to:

1. _____

2. _____

3. _____

Passion

The skills and proficiencies that you are most passionate about sometimes trump all the others.

Mentor: List three skills or areas of expertise that you are passionate about demonstrating.
Mentee: List three skills or areas of expertise that you are passionate about learning.

1. _____

2. _____

3. _____

Your passions will extend far beyond your cubicle or office walls. Maybe you're an amazing pianist, have extensive knowledge about classical music or could easily be called the Dog Whisperer. Those skills are also well worth teaching and learning and help the mentoring relationship become fuller and more balanced.

As you answer the following questions, it will help you to home in on the skills and proficiencies that you exhibit or want to learn (possibly) outside of the workplace.

1. When you're reading or talking about _____, time flies and hours feel like mere minutes.

2. You would happily get up early on a weekend to _____
   _____.

3. If you didn't have to earn an income, you'd spend your time _____
   _____.

You might find yourself mentoring or being mentored because of your all-around life passions.

Lastly, Confidence Counts

Mentors, oftentimes you know that you are strong and talented in an area but might doubt your ability to effectively transfer the skill. It's important to gauge your confidence in your ability to do so, especially if you are somewhat new to being a mentor. If you have some hesitations as to your knowledge base, you can shore that up by adding personal learning opportunities. If you have hesitations as to your ability to transfer the skill, then you might wish to practice with a mentor or peer to increase self-assurance and receive helpful feedback.

Next, you'll assess your confidence level in your subject matter knowledge and ability to teach this skill. (Choose one of your proficiencies. For example, your Pragmatics strength is creating a marketing pitch. You rate yourself 8 in confidence of your ability to teach your mentee how to do it.) Rate yourself below:

My subject matter knowledge: _____
_____

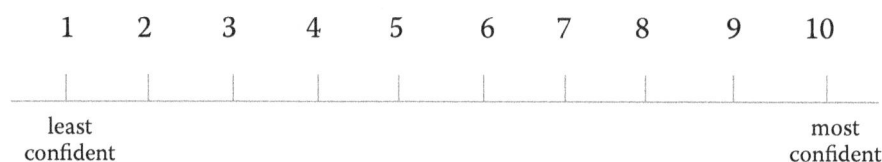

```
 1    2    3    4    5    6    7    8    9   10
 |    |    |    |    |    |    |    |    |    |
least                                    most
confident                                confident
```

Augie ArguMentor

"I'm 100% confident I can win any argument and teach my mentees to do the same! It's all about openings and rebuttals!"

What continued education, skills training or experience might you consider that strengthens your own skill level in these areas?

Have you mentored in these areas previously? If so, what was particularly successful? What skills and/or methods didn't transfer as well?

> Good mentoring happens when the mentor is clear on what they have to offer and the mentee is equally clear on what they are seeking to gain.

Know Yourself

Last month James called me with his big announcement and a request.

"Hey Lori, guess what? I'm going to write my first novel. Can you tell me how to get started and what I should do to get it on the New York Times Bestseller List?"

I smiled as I listened to the excitement in his voice, remembering my own excitement at his stage of the journey.

"Sure James, let's get together for a cup of coffee and talk about first steps. I can definitely help you with things like how to write great stories well and put some personality into your characters.

I can also give some guidance on where to find good speaking engagements to showcase your work once it's finished."

"Great! Can you also help me put my social media plan together? Everyone says I need to get on that pronto."

This time I laughed. "Nope, not the right person for that. But I know someone you can call who's an expert in social media. She can show you how to put together an integrated plan and teach you all the nuances of when and what to post so you reach the broadest audience."

"Wow, that would be great. Did you enjoy your writing and publishing journey?"

"James, let's change that cup of coffee to a glass of wine and I can give you the real scoop. You're going to have LOTS of fun!"

I hung up feeling great about James' new exploit and our conversation. I had offered to mentor in my areas of strength and then given him resources to pursue that would serve him well in my challenge areas.

When we meet I'll have to remember to tell James to keep his dog around while he writes—he might need a wiggly, joyful reminder of his strengths!

Adam AchieveMentor

"I'm confident I can help my mentees set goals they can achieve. No sense to argue, Augie, when you can make it a win-win for everyone!"

MODULE 4	SHIFT MATRIX (Example)	
	What Can I Teach and Model?	Where Do I Want to Learn and Grow?
	Mentor	**Mentee**

S Share
• Mentor: Which of the proficiencies do you feel you can best model/ transfer?
• Mentee: Which of the proficiencies are you seeking to observe/ learn?
	• *Pragmatics*
	  • *Presentation tips/guidelines*
	• *Position*
	  • *I can share what the true job requirements are for my position*
		• *Pragmatics*
		  • *Answering questions in a negotiation*
		• *Presence*
		  • *when delivering presentations*
		  • *when making my point in a meeting*

H How • How have I seen one of the proficiencies in my work and life?	• *Passion in dealing with my kids and teaching them how to avoid troublesome peers at school* • *Passion in getting the new client on board*	• *Pragmatics – I learned how to write preparatory points for a contract negotiation over the past few months*
I Insight • Why is knowing your current or desired strength important? Give an example.	• *I could focus on sharing where I'm strong e.g. closing deals*	• *I could focus on learning how to conduct and close a contract settlement* • *I wouldn't spend as much time trying to improve one of my challenge areas i.e. technical writing, since I have a team that does that for us*
F* Focus in • What is one tangible Pragmatics priority I am working on, will be working on or would like to be working on?	• *I'm closing a deal with a major customer by first quarter of next year*	• *I'm managing a mid-size contract and negotiating changes to it over the next three months. I'd like to lead a major contract negotiation within the next six months.*
T Task/Time • What date will we begin to work on our Planning Horizon for our observable events?	• *By Oct 11, next meeting*	• *By Oct 11, next meeting*

*This Pragmatics Project will flow through the process in your upcoming modules.
Key Step 1 Thought: After discussing both mentor and mentee Pragmatics priority, zero in on one that will be specific, relevant and meaningful to the mentee's goals.

MODULE 4	SHIFT MATRIX	
	What Can I Teach and Model?	Where Do I Want to Learn and Grow?
	Mentor	**Mentee**
S Share • Mentor: Which of the proficiencies do you feel you can best model/ transfer? • Mentee: Which of the proficiencies are you seeking to observe/ learn?		
H How • How have I seen one of the proficiencies in my work and life?		
I Insight • Why is knowing your current or desired strength important? Give an example.		
F* Focus in • What is one tangible Pragmatics priority I am working on, will be working on or would like to be working on?		
T Task/Time • What date will we begin to work on our Planning Horizon for our observable events?		

*This Pragmatics Project will flow through the process in your upcoming modules.
Key Step 1 Thought: After discussing both mentor and mentee Pragmatics priority, zero in on one that will be specific, relevant and meaningful to the mentee's goals.

MentorShift Roadmap
Four Step Process

Go
"Results–Track–Celebrate"

_____

_____

_____

Grow
"Challenge/Growth Areas"

_____

_____

_____

Show
"With Experiences"

_____

_____

_____

Know
"Project Definition"

_____

_____

_____

_____

KNOW Example:*

By close of this calendar year, I will lead a major contract negotiation to include leading the team, creating our positions and researching rebuttal points, developing closing arguments and presenting outcomes to senior management.

*When developing a project definition, avoid generalities such as "I will better understand..." or "I will grow in knowledge..." Those goals are difficult to measure. Instead be specific, time-bound and measurable. (*MentorShift*, Chap 21)

Summary and What's Next

As a mentor, you need to know where you are strong and most able to confidently transfer skills. Through a thoughtful examination of The Five Powerful Proficiencies™, you can better grasp where and how you'll proceed. As a mentee, you need to know what you most want to learn and experience from your mentor.

In Module 5, you will take the second MentorShift step, SHOW, "I Do, You Contribute."

Step 2: SHOW
"I Do, You Contribute"

The Power of "With"

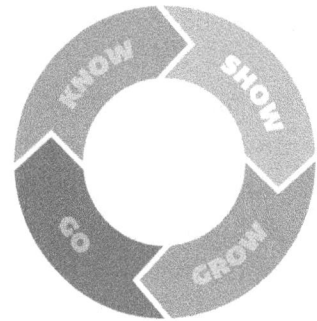

*"As I grow older, I pay less attention to what men say.
I just watch what they do."*

Andrew Carnegie, philanthropist

"Do you think the fish will be biting today, Dad?" Five-year-old Jason squinted his eyes as he surveyed the still lake that mirrored the early morning sunrise, and pulled his baseball cap low over his brow. This was important business he and his dad were doing, for not just everyone could find and outsmart cagey fish. He riveted his gaze on the motionless lake like a young pirate searching for buried treasure, hoping to sight a quick bubble or movement in an otherwise motionless surface.

"This could be a big day for us, son. I'm glad you're my fishing buddy. This is a perfect morning and extra special because we got away from our campsite without waking up your mom." Mark Clark, an experienced fisherman, delighted in these early outings with his young son. He knew

Jason did not yet have the strength to haul in a big catch or the manual dexterity to tie a line just right, so he basked in the opportunity to show him the basics of fishing. Jason could hold the pole, listen as his dad strategized about the best place to cast a line, and most importantly, he could watch and learn.

"See buddy, I'm tying this line really tight. You know these sneaky devils are surprisingly strong and this line can be surprisingly weak, so it's important to make it nice and tight."

Jason stood up and grabbed a couple of rocks to skip across the lake. "Hey, pal," his dad corrected, "hang on to those rocks and don't throw them into the water. That will scare away our little friends for sure."

Jason plunked the rocks down on the ground and sat back down beside his dad, studying the neatly organized contents of the tackle box. He watched as Mark chose just the right bright red fly, deftly tied it to the hook, stood up, and cast it across the water. A few minutes later, Mark said, "Jason, quick, we've got a hungry one! Grab that net and let's see what breakfast might look like."

Jason held tight to the net as his dad finessed the wiggly, flippery fish into it. After a minute of deliberate discussion, Dad and Jason decided this lucky Nemo was one to release.

"Son, watch how I take the hook out and put him back in the water." Mark slowly put the fish back underwater for a few moments and held it there to allow it gentle entrance back into the water.

"Did you see how calmly I put him back, Jason? This was the big event of his day and it's important to let him ease back into his environment."

"Dad, I know I can do this someday. I'm going to catch the biggest fish ever."

"Tell you what, buddy. When we get home I'll buy you a pole just your size and you can practice some casting in our driveway. It won't be long till you will be reeling them in."

"Okay, Dad, and let's tell Mom we caught 20-pounder!"

Mark laughed and looked at his boy. "Buddy, that's called a 'fish tale.' I know you're on your way because all great fishermen learn how to tell great fish tales!"

My friend, Jason, recounted this story of one of many fishing expeditions with his father as we discussed the power of observation. As a young boy, he had observed and learned. Today he'd like to say he's "bass pro" of the western U.S., but that wouldn't be true. What he can say is that from watching his own dad take him through the rudiments of a beloved pastime, in his adulthood he's a skillful fisherman who still enjoys every element of the sport.

And he invites others to watch and learn from him.

Jason's story represents the essence of Step 2: SHOW, "I Do, You Contribute." His dad was the fisherman par excellence, invited him to watch carefully and gave Jason some jobs to do to begin to hone his skills as a fisherman in the making.

The Power of Observation

How observation changes us socially

Social psychologist Albert Bandura's study of how observational learning impacts behavior still stands as one of the classic experiments in learning. Bandura's theory, known as observational or social learning, offers convincing proof that individuals can learn new information and behaviors simply by watching someone else do something and observing the consequences of their behavior.

In Bandura's famous "Bobo Doll" experiment, he set about studying how daycare center children would respond after observing an adult model punching, kicking, and yelling at the inflatable, bounce-back Bobo Doll.

Sometimes the adult was rewarded for their behavior, other times punished. After watching this, the children were put in the testing room with the Bobo Doll and their actions observed.

Bandura found the children were more likely to imitate the adult model by pummeling poor Bobo if:

- They had *observed* the aggressive behavior (versus a control group of children that didn't observe it)

- The adult was an attractive authority figure

- The adult was positively reinforced afterwards

He also found that if the adult model was negatively reinforced (punished) the children were less likely to imitate them, suggesting that:

- A step of reasoning had entered in ("Oh no, she got in trouble for hitting the clown.")

- They weighed the potential negative consequences ("I might get in trouble, too.")

- They could choose *not* to imitate ("I'm not going to hit that clown.")

We are social creatures, and not unlike the kids in the Bandura experiment. We observe others' actions and then we make a judgment—do I want to do what they did or not?

Observational learning has big implications when it comes to mentoring.

Anthony DiVittorio, a charismatic, tattooed, up-from-the-streets youth counselor has harnessed the power of observational and social learning in a big way. For years, he had witnessed the pervasive violent crimes committed by teenage boys in Chicago's inner city and wanted to help turn that tide.

To meet this problem head on, Tony founded the Becoming a Man, or BAM, program. In partnership with Youth Guidance and World Sport Chicago, BAM mentors middle and high school boys through character-building group sessions with BAM counselors during school hours. After school, the teens are trained in Olympic sports by BAM-trained coaches, including archery, martial arts, and wrestling—activities few had experienced.

DiVittorio emphasizes, "There is not a standardized rite of passage that moves a boy into manhood … so they are creating their own manhood, constantly observing, looking at role models."[1] Another BAM counselor shares, "[The boys] have a sense of identity that has to be nurtured through seeing other men. When young men have an opportunity to see role models, that's what they cling to."[2]

So how does the learning happen? They consistently observed:

- Tough, compassionate mentors willing to spend time teaching them core values of manhood—integrity, accountability, visionary goal-setting

- Men with open doors and open hearts to listen and talk about hard truths

- Men who shared about the "softer" side of life—how to treat a woman with respect, how to hold a baby, how to be a strong leader of a family

Fortunately, BAM's results have been measured. In 2009, the University of Chicago Crime Lab conducted a one-year baseline study with about 800 of the disadvantaged boys involved in the program. They had missed roughly eight weeks of school, carried a D+ average, and most had no father figure in their home. Many had lost someone close to them through gang violence. The study compared them to students with similar backgrounds who were not involved—a control group.

The study showed that participation in BAM reduced violent crime arrests by 44 percent and 36 percent for other (non-violent, non-property, non-drug) crimes. By the end of the program, the University estimates that participants had a 23-percent greater chance of graduating than those in the control group.[3]

By observing the actions and attitudes of their mentors (and one another) during the program, were these students favorably impacted? The proof is in the pudding. BAM is a powerful example of observational learning that indeed influences social behavior.

Note: Today, the BAM program touches the lives of more than 2,500 young men of color in 48 schools in 33 Chicago communities.[4] It's worth viewing a BAM video to see this social learning in action. On YouTube, type in BAM—Sports Edition[5].

How observation changes us emotionally

Conductor Benjamin Zander strides confidently across the stage in his blue jeans and sneakers as he prepares to open his famous TED talk. The wizened 70-year-old leader of the Boston Philharmonic Orchestra greets the audience, with a face poised in adoring anticipation, and begins his topic with a larger -than-life gravitas and smile. Ben Zander believes in the healing power of classical music and fervently vows that deep down, everyone loves classical music... They just might not know it yet. His presentation is "The Transformative Power of Classical Music" and his infectious passion brings a clear message throughout the 20-minute talk; not just that we all have an untapped love of classical music, but that we have an untapped love for all new possibilities and connections.

Zander moves across the stage, laughing and cajoling his audience to listen as he plays the piano as a seven-year-old would play. Then he instantly transforms into the consummate artist as he plays a moving rendition of Chopin Prelude 4 in E Minor, Op. 28. He urges his audience to listen to it as they quietly and fondly remember a lost love.

As the camera moves in for a close-up shot of Zander's hands moving magically over the keyboard, he is at once a sculptor, inventor, masseuse, and healer. The audience sits enraptured.

He ends his presentation by beseeching his listeners with questions like "Is who you are someone who will bring light into another person's eyes?"

With his music, energy, and vulnerability, he transports the audience from tears to joyous laughter; as he bounds energetically across the stage and out into the audience, he becomes one with the rhythm and heartbeat of the audience, offering a warm touch or holding someone's hand.

As I watched, his scintillating performance held me spellbound.

I had to see it. Experience it. The power was not just his in words. I could have read words in the TED transcript after his performance. The power was in his persona and all of the non-verbal impressions that flooded and flowed over the 1,600 audience members.

It was the magic that I observed—the privilege I enjoyed that came from just watching him. Observing him gave me a gift that no second-hand story, no transcript could ever offer.

I finished watching the zealous Mr. Zander and walked thoughtfully to my kitchen, poured a cup of hot tea, turned on Vivaldi's "Four Seasons," and sat back in my chair with a deep breath of appreciation.

Observation had an emotional influence, and this is exactly the point. It was the experience of observing his actions, passion, and giftedness that impacted me.

How observation changes us physiologically

Here are a few interesting, if not offbeat, facts about your brain.

- It is about the size of a cantaloupe, has about the same consistency as tofu and weighs close to 3 pounds

- *Sphenopalatine ganglioneuralgia* is the scientific term for "brain freeze"[6]

- When awake, the human brain produces enough electricity to power a small light bulb[7]

Now on to a few more relevant brain facts.

- You were born with at least a 100 billion neurons in your brain[8]

- New brain connections are created every time you form a memory

- Your brain has a "plasticity" to it that allows it to learn and keep learning

Your brain captures and holds on to new information through the following process.

Brain cells are called neurons. They have the ability to grow dendrites when you learn something new, like branches on a tree. The more you practice what you have learned, the more the dendrites spread out and become stronger and thicker. The thicker the dendrites, the faster the information flows. So repeating an action, be it watching, listening, or physically doing something, builds a connection that lasts a very long time.

And you remember what you have learned!

What does this have to do with mentoring? It underscores the importance of repeatedly observing what your mentor does that you desire to learn. Repeated observation in essence hardcodes it into your brain, to be retained for future use.

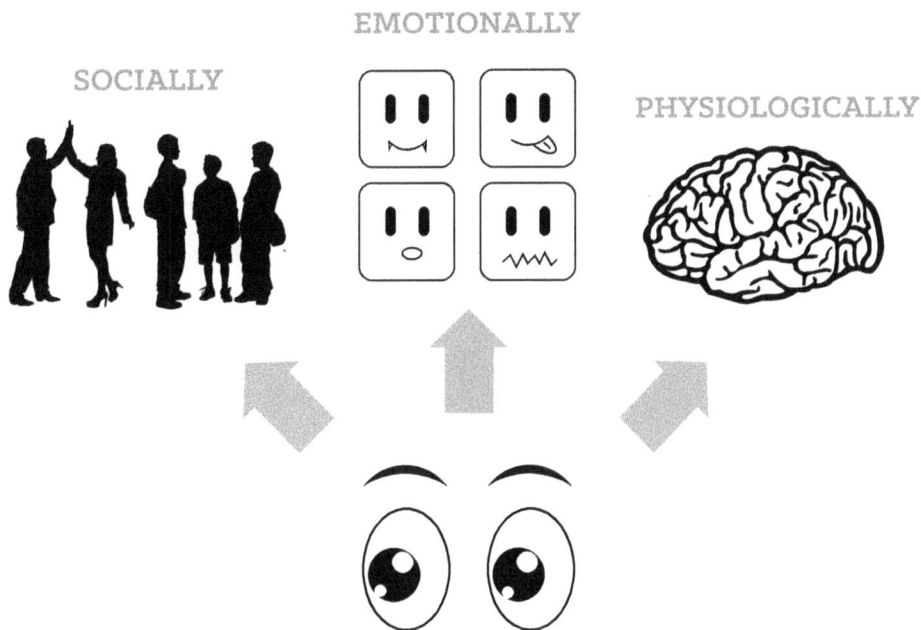

Observation Influences You

Observation in Your Life

In Step 2: SHOW, you want to intentionally and creatively move away from the conference room and out into your world, where a mentee can observe their mentor in action. We'll begin with some questions to get you thinking about the power of observation in your life.

Mentor and Mentee: Thinking back on your personal and professional life, what are three valuable skills that you would have had a hard time mastering without first seeing them performed by someone else?

Example—Driving a car or riding a bike

1. _____

2. _____

3. _____

Describe a time when someone asked you to accomplish a task without first letting you observe them doing and explaining it. What was the result?

Example: Asking a subordinate to present material to your boss without prepping them or including them in a prior discussion with the boss

_____

_____

_____

_____

Briefly summarize something that you've learned from someone, that you could never have learned in an office or conference room.

Example: Effective networking at a company social

_____

_____

_____

_____

Observation PLUS Contribution

Former major league baseball player, Sam Ewing, once said, "Hard work spotlights the character of people: some turn up their sleeves, some turn up their noses, and some don't turn up at all." I know right here and now that every mentee reading this is a "turn up your sleeves" kind of person and is eager to jump in and contribute on their Pragmatics Project in a big way.

That's great, because Step 2, SHOW, is "I Do, You Contribute." Research shows that learning happens most effectively when you learn experientially, i.e., learning by doing. Roger C. Schank, one of the world's leading visionaries in learning theory and cognitive science, in his article, "What We Learn When We Learn by Doing" illustrates the point this way:

"How do we enhance learning? One way to enhance learning is by doing. If you want to learn about food and wine you have to eat and drink. If you want to learn how to drive, you have to drive. If you want to learn to fly a plane, you need to, at least, fly a simulated plane.

What does this tell us about training and education then? It tells us… we need to transform all training and education so that it looks, feels, and is like doing."[9]

Observation is a critical component of mentoring, but it can't stop there. Mentees need to "turn up their sleeves" and become actively involved in the learning process.

What if you only watched your colleague create a terrific financial analysis, but never did one yourself? What if you observed your mentor leading a team effort, but didn't take part?

Of course, you'd be losing out. Learning by doing brings you these important benefits:

- Participation

- Interaction

- Contact with real-world environments

- Whole-person learning (visual, auditory, kinesthetic)

Learning by doing has big implications
when it comes to mentoring.

In Step 2, SHOW, the SHIFT Matrix encourages conversation about where and when the mentor can invite the mentee to observe so the mentee receives maximum opportunity for learning. It is here that you plan your "with" experiences (Chapters 30, 31 *MentorShift*), which capitalize on observational and learning by doing activities.

In addition, in this module we introduce the Planning Horizon. It is your first step toward making a timeline for these observable "with" events in any of the Five Powerful Proficiencies. As you walk through the Planning Horizon together, under the Pragmatic proficiency, be sure to include planned "Contributions" by the mentee for the events/activities that would benefit them.

Emma EnjoyMentor

"Creating a project together sounds fun and it will help a mentee gain great new skills. Wouldn't you agree, Augie?"

Learning by Doing: Focusing in on Your "Pragmatics Project"

In this module, mentors and mentees dive deeper into their Pragmatics project, which allows the mentor to demonstrate desired behaviors and the mentee to learn and take increased responsibility over time. In Step 3, GROW, the mentee's responsibility and contribution will increase even further.

At this point, I want to emphasize two words that will make your mentoring different from the other models you might have experienced. The best two words to solve the "Yakking, Tracking, Get Sent Packing" model and ensure great "with" experiences are...

Mentor = INVITE   **Mentee = ASK**

Keep this at top of mind! Mentor, whenever possible, think of an experience that you can invite your mentee to join in. Mentee, ask whenever you think of an observable event in which you'd like to join your mentor.

Ask yourself:

"When, where and how" can we go and do something together that will move this project forward?"

- Visit a customer together?

- Walk a shop floor or assembly line and analyze the process?

- Negotiate with a vendor together?

Mentor/Mentee: Each list two "with" activities/events that mentor can invite mentee to where they will demonstrate/model desired behaviors and where the mentee can contribute to help further the project along.

With Activity (observable event)

Examples: Mentor invites mentee to meeting with customer; mentee asks to accompany mentor to tour of their manufacturing facility

#1 _____

_____

#2 _____

_____

Mentor/Mentee: For each "with" activity you listed, write a sentence that summarizes how it could benefit mentee.

#1 _____

_____

#2 _____

_____

Augie ArguMentor

"I'd argue that the mentee needs a dozen projects so they can exponentially increase their learning. Research shows that the human brain can handle a multitude of tasks. Let's add on a few more."

Your answers to these questions will prepare you to complete the upcoming SHIFT Matrix together.

We will assume for "Example" purposes going forward that the mentee has chosen, "Lead a Major Contract Negotiation" as their Pragmatic Project. The following examples in Modules 5 through 8 will follow that assumption.

Learning by Doing: Planning the Other Proficiencies

In addition to the Pragmatics Project, mentor and mentee will be planning out activities to incorporate the other four Ps—Passporting, Presence, Position, and Passion. These are not as discrete and measurable as progress with a Pragmatic Project is; nevertheless, planning how to benefit from these other broader mentoring opportunities is essential.

Emma EnjoyMentor

"Augie, I think you need to chill."

MODULE 5	SHIFT MATRIX (Example)	
	Where Will I Invite My Mentee?	What Do I Want to Observe or Experience?
	Pragmatics Project: To lead a major contract negotiation	
	Mentor	**Mentee**
S* **Share** • Mentor: What upcoming events, meetings or activities might benefit your mentee? • Mentee: What would you like to see or experience?	• *I have a large negotiation to conduct next month* • *I will be speaking to an industry-wide Contracts group in two months*	• *I'd like to make connections with Marketing and Engineering leads. I use their material greatly in the proposals I develop and I can connect with them on negotiation points when it is time to do so*
H **How** • How can the events that you listed support the mentee's goals?	• *I have contacts in Marketing and Engineering that I can introduce him to* • *He can observe my industry-wide Contracts presentation and the type of content I share*	• *Meeting experts in these two areas will benefit my negotiation strategies and presentation*
I **Insight** • What activities that are not in the workplace might you do together?	• *I read two to three business books a month; we could meet for coffee and talk about one he's interested in* • *I play golf and like to watch sporting events*	• *I'm a Broncos fan and can snag tickets to an occasional home game* • *I'm a techno junkie so I am really familiar with all things related to computers so could do some reverse mentoring to help my mentor set up or maintain their system*
F **Focus in** • Mentor and mentee: What could derail the plans you make together?	• *Possibly the customer might not want me to bring someone else along, however, I will do my best to work on that issue*	• *I have to travel quite a bit for work so it could cause some rescheduling*
T **Task/Time** • When will we have our timephased Planning Horizon started? Completed?	• *Start next week at our meeting* • *Finish by end of the month*	• *Start next week at our meeting* • *Finish by end of the month*

*Key Step 2 Thought:
• Mentor—How will you practice "with" mentoring by <u>inviting</u> your mentee to go with you?
• Mentee—How will you practice "with" mentoring by <u>asking</u> your mentor to take you with them?

MODULE 5	SHIFT MATRIX	
	Where Will I Invite My Mentee?	What Do I Want to Observe or Experience?
	Pragmatics Project:	
	Mentor	**Mentee**
S* **Share** • Mentor: What upcoming events, meetings or activities, might benefit your mentee? • Mentee: What would you like to see or experience?		
H **How** • How can the events that you listed support the mentee's goals?		
I **Insight** • What activities that are not in the workplace might you do together?		
F **Focus in** • Mentor and mentee: What could derail the plans you make together?		
T **Task/Time** • When will we have our timephased Planning Horizon started? Completed?		

*Key Step 2 Thought:
- Mentor—How will you practice "with" mentoring by <u>inviting</u> your mentee to go with you?
- Mentee—How will you practice "with" mentoring by <u>asking</u> your mentor to take you with them?

REVIEW
The Five Powerful Proficiencies™ of a Mentor

1. Pragmatics

A specific skill that includes practical how-to expertise, such as building a cohesive team, writing software code, analyzing a financial document or delivering a great presentation.

2. Passporting

You can strengthen your mentee's network by introducing them to people that can help them reach their goals. Every mentor can benefit a mentee by offering introductions and some of you will be especially gifted passporters.

3. Presence

You command a presence just by being in the room, and can offer an impressive example of how to handle authority and opposition.

4. Position

You hold a position that the mentee aspires to or wants to learn more about.

If you mentor because of your position, you will reveal your real job description played out in real life.

PRAGMATICS
Specific, practical how-tos

PASSPORTING
Making introductions, building a network

PRESENCE
Handling authority, dealing with opposition

POSITION
Real job description in real life

PASSION
Model inner motivation that drives success

The Five Powerful Proficiencies™ in a Mentor

5. Passion

You are passionate about your work and demonstrate how that inner fire can support your success.

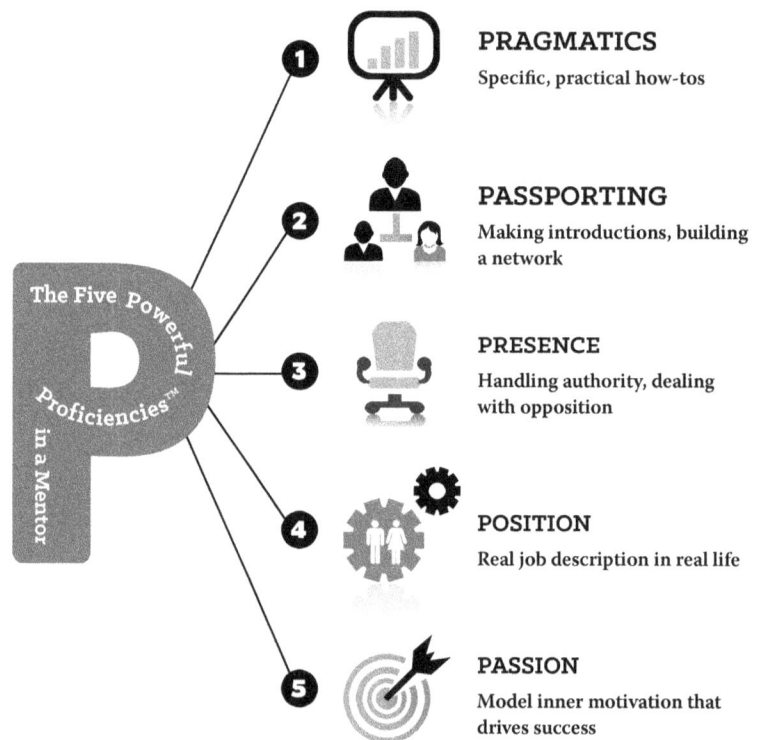

Now that you have identified observable events, you can PLAN TOGETHER:

- What will happen

- When it will happen

- Potential mentee contributions

When you undertake the Planning Horizon, brainstorm which activities/events/meetings you'd like to shoot for and set the target date together. Your Planning Horizon will likely have changes as you move through time, but the important thing is to set a schedule with milestones. It increases accountability and potential for success.

STEP 2: SHOW—"I Do, You Contribute"

PRAGMATICS—PLANNING HORIZON
EXAMPLE

PRAGMATICS PROJECT: Lead a major contract negotiation

	January	Date	February	Date	March	Date	April	Date
Pragmatics	Discussion: How to set up contracts terms and conditions; objectives	1/15	Walk through contract details	2/25	Invite to contract negotiation/ debrief *	3/20	Walk through Best and Final Offer/debrief;	4/10
Step 2 Contribution	Ask questions		Suggestions on contract details		Assist in prep		Assist in materials prep and debrief	

*Note that the observable events might occur outside of the workplace

STEP 2: SHOW, "I Do, You Contribute"

PRAGMATICS—PLANNING HORIZON

PRAGMATICS PROJECT:

	January	Date	February	Date	March	Date	April	Date
Pragmatics								
Step 2 Contribution								

	May	Date	June	Date	July	Date	August	Date
Pragmatics								
Step 2 Contribution								

	September	Date	October	Date	November	Date	December	Date
Pragmatics								
Step 2 Contribution								

Note that the observable events might occur outside of the workplace

STEP 2: SHOW, "I Do, You Contribute"

Passporting, Presence, Position, Passion
PLANNING HORIZON EXAMPLE

PRAGMATICS PROJECT: Lead a major contract negotiation

	January	Date	February	Date	March	Date	April	Date
Passport	Intro to Director Engineering Intro to Director Marketing	1/30	Networking event down-town*	2/15	Company X arrives in house; make introductions	3/14		
Presence			Invite to next level mgt. con-tract/debrief	2/30			Invite to mentor presentation to senior mgt.	4/12
Position	Explanation of job description/ Dept interfaces	1/15	Discussion past roadblocks/ challenges	2/4	Invite to staff meeting	3/4	Invite on trip to visit customer	4/30
Passion					Company seats at basketball game *	3/11		

*Note that the observable events might span outside of the workplace

** Note that you will be adding the mentee's contribution for the Pragmatics Project but not the other four: Passport, Presence, Position, and Passion. As you might expect, it's difficult to measure contribution with some of the more intangible elements of mentoring.

STEP 2: SHOW, "I Do, You Contribute"

Passporting, Presence, Position, Passion
PLANNING HORIZON EXAMPLE

PRAGMATICS PROJECT:

	January	Date	February	Date	March	Date	April	Date
Passport								
Presence								
Position								
Passion								

	May	Date	June	Date	July	Date	August	Date
Passport								
Presence								
Position								
Passion								

	September	Date	October	Date	November	Date	December	Date
Passport								
Presence								
Position								
Passion								

*Note that the observable events might occur outside of the workplace

** Note that you will be adding the mentee's contribution for the Pragmatics Project but not the other four: Passport, Presence, Position, and Passion. As you might expect, it's difficult to measure contribution with some of the more intangible elements of mentoring.

MentorShift Roadmap
Four Step Process

Go
"Results—Track—Celebrate"

_____

_____

_____

Grow
"Challenge/Growth Areas"

_____

_____

_____

Show
"With Experiences"

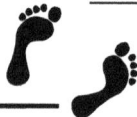

_____

_____

_____

_____

Know
"Project Definition"

_____

_____

_____

_____

SHOW Example:*

I will ask my mentor to accompany them to their upcoming contract presentation and to one smaller negotiation. I will ask to attend the contracts conference next month with my mentor.

*When choosing "with" activities, both mentor and mentee brainstorm creative ideas that would support the mentee's learning and involvement, both at and away from the office.

84

Summary and What's Next

Step 2, SHOW is chiefly about invitation and observation. Plan together what events or activities you can do with each other at the office, and ones that take you occasionally outside of the office.

Mentor—**INVITE** your mentee to go with you!

Mentee—**ASK** to accompany your mentor!

Harness the Power of **WITH**!

In Module 6, you will see how the mentee takes on more and more responsibility, and you'll measure your results.

Step 3: GROW
"You Do, I Contribute"

The Power of Learning by Doing

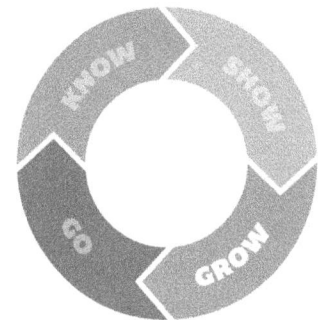

". . . .to learn and not to do is really not to learn."

Stephen Covey, leadership expert

I remember sitting in my high school sophomore year Algebra class, staring out the window as I doodled lazily on my notebook, and wondering, "When and how will I *ever* use this stuff?" I couldn't imagine how this subject matter would have any relationship to the exciting life adventures that surely lay in my future. (As it turns out, a career in aerospace finance working with every kind of engineer known to humankind caused those algebra factoids to come in pretty handy.)

I bet you can relate to my contemplative search for "book-learning meaning." Like mine, your educational experience at times meant 2-pound textbooks, "multiple guess" tests, and pop quizzes. You waited till you launched from the hallowed halls of your academic institution to find out what it all actually means in *real life*.

In his recent *Wired* article, "American Schools Are Training Kids for a World That Doesn't Exist," Harvard professor, David Edwards, expresses this quandary as such,

> "To become a chef, a lawyer, a philosopher or an engineer, has always been a matter of learning what these professionals do, how and why they do it, and some set of general facts that more or less describe our societies and ourselves. We pass from kindergarten through twelfth grade, from high school to college, from college to graduate and professional schools, ending our education at some predetermined stage to become the chef, or the engineer, equipped with a fair understanding of what being a chef, or an engineer, actually is and will be for a long time. **We learn, and after[wards], we do. We go to school and then we go to work.**
>
> This approach does not map very well to personal and professional success in America today. Learning and doing have become inseparable in the face of conditions that invite us to discover."[1]

Edwards goes on to describe those invitations to discovery through "learning by doing" experiences like those conducted by his fellow Harvard educators. In a few examples these professors:

- Ask the students to make films to understand science

- Bring students to low income regions to learn about social entrepreneurship

- Invite master chefs to help students discover the science of cooking

- Teach aesthetics by inviting students to use performing and visual art to effect social and political change

In all of these examples, the students are fully involved, from head to toe, both mind and body. They are rolling up their sleeves and getting to work, real-time.

Edwards is on to something profound but not entirely new. His emphasis on discovery through "learning by doing" feels like a breath of fresh air, but it is not really different at all, in fact, it is an old and time-proven principle: *Deep learning occurs when you dynamically engage, when you discover through creative, practice-based action.*

And why shouldn't this timeless principle apply to your mentoring all the more?

Learning by Doing—What's the Mentoring Difference?

Grabbing ahold of this learning by doing philosophy and practice of MentorShift's Step 2, SHOW and Step 3, GROW separates those who remain mentoring novices from those who go on to mentor masterfully. You now take a leap in your thinking that moves you away from the comfortable conference table (the business equivalent of two-pound textbooks, "multiple guess" tests and pop quizzes) and out into the real world. You progress from the mentoring default of reading the business book *du jour* and talking about it together to actually sculpting what you really want to teach and learn.

You are busy with so many important things in your life that you will want to ensure your mentoring relationship does the important stuff in the most effective, lasting way. In Step 2 and 3, you *create, customize and craft* your mentoring relationship. It won't look like anyone else's.

You might be thinking, "I don't have time to do that, just give me the business book to read with my mentee." I believe you don't have time *not* to create a meaningful roadmap together, that is, not if you're serious about passing on career or life skills.

Dayna Drive-ByMentor

"This project Step 3 stuff is a piece of cake! Swoop in, toss out a few pearls of wisdom, and off to the next venture!"

Let's dig deeper into the most powerful way to optimize learning for all involved.

Learning by Doing—Serial Planning versus Parallel Planning

In MentorShift, good planning for your learning experience sets the stage for success. You will plan learning opportunities in a couple of ways, both illustrated below:

When aerospace workers build a satellite, they plan and perform some tasks "serially" and some tasks "in parallel."

For example, test engineers conduct rigorous *serial* procedures when verifying spacecraft hardware because it's critical that the test is run *in a prescribed order*. For example, when testing the level of shock that a satellite structure could endure in flight, the test engineers might perform a test like this: "Drop 1" occurs from a certain height, "Drop 2" from a slightly increased height, and so forth. Then each step is measured as to its shock effect on the satellite. The test runs

Dan DevelopMentor

"Learning a new process can take some time. Mentees need patient coaching, wouldn't you agree? Dayna? Hmmm, She was here a minute ago..."

serially, each with increasing impact. If the tests were conducted with steps missing or out of order, the analysts would lose critical data.

Spacecraft work also occurs *in parallel*. At any given time you might not only observe the same test engineers running the shock test above, you might see a cordoned off factory section for wiring cables, one for assembling subcomponents and another for cleaning the finished product. As several satellites move through these stations, the work is performed in parallel, *at the same time.*

I offer a more downhome example of working serially and in parallel. When I make my world-famous lasagna (I hate to brag...well, not really), serially, I cut up the tomatoes first, then the mushrooms, then the garlic bulbs before I start the sauce.

In parallel, I sizzle the hot Italian sausage as I assemble my tomato sauce ingredients. As my tomato sauce simmers, I boil the noodles. As I deftly layer the Parmesan and mozzarella cheese with the noodles in the pan, I sip a glass of fine Italian wine. (I can do so many important things at one time.)

You see how it goes and the same holds true for mentoring.

Mentoring includes both serial and parallel planning. For instance, your mentor is showing you how to create a great marketing campaign—first you assess your addressable market, then what market you can capture, then what your competitor is doing. (serial) At the same time, you and she are working to contact advertisers, buy ad space, and negotiate terms and conditions with the printing house. (in parallel)

The Five P's Planning Horizon helps you plan both serial and parallel activities and events across a broad range of your interests so you can learn most fully.

Learning by Doing—When does the Mentee Take on More Responsibility and Leadership?

In Step 2, SHOW, the mentor has the lead. In Step 3, GROW, the baton is passed to the mentee to a large degree. But mentor, how will you know the right time for your mentee to assume more responsibility? Mentee, how will you know when you are ready to begin leading much more of the task?

This can indeed feel like a mysterious question in mentoring but MentorShift has a process to guide you. Two main factors guide Step 3 timing and the increase in responsibility and leadership:

1. **The mentee's skill level/experience base with regard to the Pragmatics project that they will lead**

2. **Demonstrated proficiency in Step 2 SHOW tasks**

The following examples show how the mentor Jayne assesses her mentees' skill levels and plans what she and her mentees need to do to properly prepare them for the project they are going to undertake.

Example #1

Pragmatics Project:

- Stephen will prepare to deliver an executive presentation, specifically the quarterly financial report to the senior leadership in his division of the company.

Mentee's skill level/experience base:

- Stephen has given a few presentations but they were short and his audience was primarily made up of his peers.

- He delivered the presentation but struggled with cadence and keeping within his allotted time.

Conclusion:

- Jayne will proceed more slowly in transferring responsibility in Step 3 tasks as Stephen builds confidence, gradually adding opportunities to practice presentations before he delivers to an executive audience.

Example #2

Pragmatics Project:

- Jon will prepare to deliver an executive presentation, specifically the quarterly financial report to the senior leadership in his division of the company.

Mentee's skill level/experience base:

- Jon has given many presentations to mid-level audiences.

- He delivered his presentations effectively and desires most to polish off his closing remarks with a powerful summary and call to action.

Conclusion:

- Jayne will proceed to transfer responsibility rather quickly in Step 3 tasks as Jon has shown strong and consistent presentation skills, needing just some refinement before an executive audience.

In moving from Step 2, SHOW, to Step 3, GROW, one size doesn't fit all. Responsibility transfers uniquely to match the skill level and readiness of the mentee.

Low Mentee Skill Level	**+**	Lower Success in Step 2 Task	**=**	<u>More</u> time to transfer skill, and a greater time commitment on behalf the mentor
High Mentee Skill Level	**+**	Higher Success in Step 2 Task	**=**	<u>Less</u> time to transfer skill, and a smaller time commitment on behalf the mentor

While both Stephen and Jon want to learn how to give effective presentations, Jayne and the mentees must assess their skills and experiences in order to provide them with the support they need.

Mentors, when you work with a mentee such as Jon, or with Stephen as he hones his skill, I encourage you to offer "stretch assignments" as you see your mentee progress. A stretch assignment offers the additional tasks and challenges that might seem a sizable reach for the mentee, but that they can accomplish through your support and feedback.

At this point you might be wondering, when does Step 2 end and Step 3 begin?

Let me start by explaining what this transition *is not*.

- It's *not* neat, clean and perfectly linear

- It's *not* a "hard stop" to Step 2 and "immediate start" to Step 3

- It's *not* entering Step 3 and never returning to Step 2

Let's go back to our Jayne and Jon illustration. Jon might proceed easily to Step 3 by assuming leadership for a total presentation to senior leadership. However, he may find that in so doing, he struggles a bit with the operational element of the presentation. So he returns to Step 2 and observes Jayne again as Jayne delivers the operational portion of the financial reports to her management. He assists Jayne with executive level summary charts and then practices with her to effectively summarize the quarterly earnings.

Jon then goes back to Step 3 and better incorporates the financial data into his presentations.

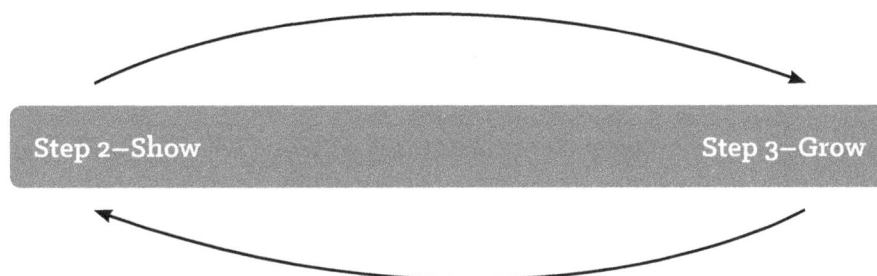

Step 2—Show	Step 3—Grow

Learning by Doing—How Can you Measure Learning?

Simply put, you can measure learning in the Pragmatic proficiency most easily. Why? Because you can be objective when it comes to pragmatics. Whatever the practical skill or craft, it is specific, with a beginning and an end and often a completed product. You can be objective such that you can rate your progress on a scale or continuum and discuss with your mentor.

When it comes to measuring growth in the other four proficiencies within the MentorShift process, that is, Passporting, Position, Presence, Passion, it's more difficult to measure objectively.

For example, you can objectively assess if you have learned the Pragmatic of how to conduct and close a sales call exemplified by your mentor. You can measure if the client is receptive and you ultimately closed the sale.

The evaluation tool at the end of this module helps you measure pragmatics. For the other four more subjective proficiencies, questions at the end foster a discussion that will help the mentee to further develop the desired proficiency.

Learning by Doing—Meeting the Mentee's Challenges

It's at this point in the MentorShift process that a mentee will want to capitalize on the support the mentor can provide in their overall growth. It's a chance for the mentee to share, in a safe and trusting environment, areas where they could really use some help they might not otherwise suggest to bosses or peers. I'm not asking for "the dirt" here, just the areas where you might have a bit of a challenge and that, through some coaching, would further the project that you are working on.

Mentee, you are learning by doing and your mentor is with you coaching and cheering you on. You have the support you need. So...

Ask yourself:

Mentee: Within this project, what is a skill you could be required to do to move your project forward and where you could benefit from your mentor's expertise, advice and input?

- What is one behavior at work I could get better at?

- What is something I am reluctant to do – for whatever reason that will be required of me as part of this project?

  o   Am I conflict averse?

  o   Am I nervous when speaking in public and don't command the attention and respect I deserve?

  o   Is there a technological aspect I don't understand

Mentor: How can you share your expertise to help your mentee grow in confidence and competence in this area?

When you've identified the area(s), let your mentor know. Then set up "with" experiences, project milestones or a discussion about ways to strengthen that area of challenge.

Mentees, in Step 3 the learning baton passes in a big way to you and soon you will be prepared to perform these tasks fully on your own. As you are taking on more and more responsibility and navigating how to do that successfully, I encourage you with the words of Steve Chandler in his book, *Reinventing Yourself: How to Become the Person You've Always Wanted to Be,* "Do it badly; do it slowly; do it fearfully; do it any way you have to, *but do it.*"

MODULE 6	SHIFT MATRIX (Example)	
	What Task Will the Mentee Take On?	What Are My Goals for This Task?
Pragmatics Project: To lead a major contract negotiation		
	Mentor	**Mentee**
S **Share** • Mentor: Discuss the tasks and decide which one the mentee will be doing.	• *Taking over the lead of the negotiation team*	• *Take over the negotiation team* • *For now, assume a larger portion of leading the current negotiations*
H **How** • How will the mentee prepare for this task?	• *Do the Opening and lead the discussion throughout the negotiation; mentor does the Closing*	• *Prepare a list of questions to ask mentor* • *Discuss specifics with mentor in how to handle a customer who won't yield their position on an issue*
I **Insight** • Mentee: What type of support would you like from your mentor? • Mentor: What type of support are you available to provide?	• *I am free to debrief after each negotiation for the next couple of months*	• *I'd like to be able to discuss the negotiation afterwards* • *I'd like to ask my mentor who in the negotiation could be my 'go-to' person on our team to help with administrative details and follow-up*
F* **Focus in** • What are the most important things for the mentee to do at this point in the project? • Mentee, what is a skill that will be required for this project that you need to improve?	• *To facilitate the negotiation so that all on our team have a chance to contribute* • *To come adequately prepared with the material and anticipating questions that might come up*	• *How to effectively talk to the team members about their roles in the prep and actual negotiation meeting; sometimes I focus only on my part and I want to prepare my team better*
T **Task/Time** • By what date will the Mentee complete this task? What check-in points (if any) are needed?	• *Mentee will take on these additional responsibilities over the next month* • *We will debrief each week as a check-in point because I will be in attendance at most of the negotiations*	• *I will be able to lead the full negotiation with my mentor present within three months*

*Key Step 3 Thought:
• Focus on a challenge area for the mentor to support and for the mentee to specifically improve while doing the Pragmatics Project.

MODULE 6	SHIFT MATRIX	
	What Task Will the Mentee Take On?	What Are My Goals for This Task?
Pragmatics Project:		
	Mentor	**Mentee**
S Share • Mentor: Discuss the tasks and decide which one the mentee will be doing.		
H How • How will the mentee prepare for this task?		
I Insight • Mentee: What type of support would you like from your mentor? • Mentor: What type of support are you available to provide?		
F* Focus in • What are the most important things for the mentee to do at this point in the project? • Mentee, what is a skill that will be required for this project that you need to improve?		
T Task/Time • By what date will the Mentee complete this task? What check-in points (if any) are needed?		

*Key Step 3 Thought:
• Focus on a challenge area for the mentor to support and for the mentee to specifically improve while doing the Pragmatics Project.

STEP 3: GROW – *"You Do, I Contribute"*

PRAGMATICS—PLANNING HORIZON
EXAMPLE

PRAGMATICS PROJECT: Lead a major contract negotiation

	January	Date	February	Date	March	Date	April	Date
Pragmatics	Discussion: How to set up contracts terms and conditions; objectives	1/15	Walk through contract details	2/25	Invite to contract negotiation/ debrief	3/20	Walk through Best and Final Offer/debrief;	4/10
Step 3 Contribution								
*Mentor Evaluation								
Mentee Evaluation								

	May	Date	June	Date	July	Date	August	Date
Pragmatics	New bid: Work on setting up contracts Ts&Cs; objectives	5/6	Negotiation process with vendor	6/12	Continued negotiation	1/30	Continued negotiation— Best and Final offer	8/20
Step 3 Contribution			Do opener: Present financials at negotiations		Create rebuttals; present rebuttals		Draft total Best and Final offer	
Mentor Evaluation			6				8	
Mentee Evaluation			6				7	

	September	Date	October	Date	November	Date	December	Date
Pragmatics	Contract settlement	9/15						
Step 3 Contribution	Lead final closing							
Mentor Evaluation	9							
Mentee Evaluation	8							

* Mentor + Mentee use this to evaluate Mentee growth and performance along the way
1-10 scale: 1 = Needs much work; 10 = Outstanding

STEP 3: GROW – *"You Do, I Contribute"*

PRAGMATICS—PLANNING HORIZON
EXAMPLE

PRAGMATICS PROJECT: Lead a major contract negotiation

	January	Date	February	Date	March	Date	April	Date
Pragmatics								
Step 3 Contribution								
*Mentor Evaluation								
Mentee Evaluation								

	May	Date	June	Date	July	Date	August	Date
Pragmatics								
Step 3 Contribution								
Mentor Evaluation								
Mentee Evaluation								

	September	Date	October	Date	November	Date	December	Date
Pragmatics								
Step 3 Contribution								
Mentor Evaluation								
Mentee Evaluation								

* Mentor + Mentee use this to evaluate Mentee growth and performance along the way

1-10 scale: 1 = Needs much work; 10 = Outstanding

REFLECTION

Passporting, Presence, Position and Passion Proficiencies

Step 3: GROW—REFLECTION: Passporting, Presence, Position & Passion

Mentees: As mentioned before, it is difficult to measure these four Proficiencies. Rather, use these assessments to reflect on your progress and your growth in these less tangible areas. Discuss your answers with your mentor after considering each.

Mentors: These assessments will help you to determine how best to help your mentee to continue developing the desired proficiency.

Passporting—Mentor can strengthen a mentee's network by introducing them to people that can help them reach their goals. Every mentor can benefit a mentee by offering introductions and some of you will be especially gifted passporters.

MENTEE:

Do you often find yourself introducing people to one another? Is this an easy thing for you to do? Why or why not?

In the course of an average week, how often do you recognize and follow through with the opportunity to introduce people who can be of service to one another?

Share this self-assessment with your mentor and discuss next steps for your continued development in Passporting.

Presence—Mentor commands a presence, just by being in the room and can offer an impressive example of how to handle authority and opposition.

MENTEE:

What traits or behaviors characterize the presence of your mentor?

_____

_____

While observing your mentor handling authority and opposition, what's most impressive to you?

_____

_____

_____

Share this self-assessment with your mentor and discuss how you can learn and develop the traits and behaviors that contribute to your mentor's powerful presence.

Position—Mentor holds a position that the mentee aspires to or wants to learn more about. If the mentor is mentoring because of their position, they will reveal their real job description played out in real life.

MENTEE:

What tasks or responsibilities have you observed your mentor doing that you didn't know were part of his or her position?

_____

_____

_____

Of everything you've observed your mentor doing as part of his or her position, what is most important for you to more fully comprehend?

_____

_____

Share this self-assessment with your mentor and discuss whether you should learn more about these tasks or responsibilities or focus on another aspect of developing your understanding and skills of their position.

Passion—Mentors are passionate about their work and demonstrate how that inner fire supports their success.

MENTEE:

List a few things that you as mentee are passionate about. Call to mind a few examples where you do a good job of demonstrating your passion(s).

_____

_____

What particular passions of your mentor inspire you most?

_____

_____

Share this self-assessment with your mentor and discuss how you can continue to grow and improve in this proficiency.

MentorShift Roadmap
Four Step Process

Go
"Results–Track–Celebrate"

Grow
"Challenge/Growth Areas"

_____
_____
_____
_____

Show
"With Experiences"

_____
_____
_____
_____

GROW Example:*

I will take on additional responsibility in my challenge area, that is, succinctly preparing an executive summary of the negotiation. I will prepare the executive summary and present it as well to senior management.

Know
"Project Definition"

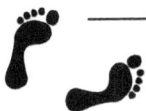

_____
_____
_____
_____

* When choosing additional responsibilities in Step 3, GROW, be sure to include those that will address and strengthen your challenge areas.

Summary and Next Steps

In Step 3, GROW, the mentee has assumed a large portion of responsibility. Soon they will be performing on their own so the mentee's active involvement is key.

In our next module, we focus on the importance and how-tos of giving and receiving effective feedback throughout Step 2, SHOW and Step 3, GROW.

Step 3: GROW (cont.) "You Do, I Contribute"

The Power of Good Feedback

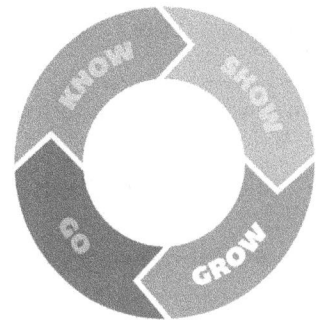

"Integrity is telling myself the truth. And honesty is telling the truth to other people."

Spencer Johnson, business author

It was the best of times and the worst of times. No, this isn't an allusion to the opening line in the Dickens classic, *Tale of Two Cities*; it's a reference to the times when I have enjoyed (or endured) the best of feedback and the worst of feedback. There's a lesson to be learned from both. Both instances occurred within my job setting at the time, and yet the lessons easily translate to mentoring relationships.

Let's begin with the worst of feedback. My boss lived and worked several hundred miles away. We spoke several times a week about the business of the day and traveled on work junkets together. We had plenty of time to discuss anything and everything related to my performance. I would read her body language and occasionally ask how she thought a presentation or project of mine had gone, but that was the beginning and end of what she had to say to me about my strengths and challenges on the job, and not a word about how I could improve.

On the prescribed day when all employees received their annual merit increase, she called and said, "Lori, I rated you 4.0 for the year [out of a 5.0 as highest on a scale] and your merit increase will reflect that. In fact, you should see it in your paycheck today. Your performance was good and you achieved some good things. Sorry I didn't talk to you sooner about your rating." And our conversation ended as she departed for a meeting.

I wasn't displeased with my rating but I was left to wonder: "Why not a 5.0? Or, for that matter, why not a 3.0?" I didn't have much to go on.

This was the worst of feedback because it needed to be:

- More specific (I heard vague rambling)

- More two-way (I heard non-helpful monologue)

- More timely (Not the moment my automatically deposited raise hit my bank account!)

- More consistent throughout the performance period (Once is not enough)

- More forward-looking ("Oops, my next appointment is waiting. Talk about future steps later.")

My best of feedback example is much more heartening. It had been an up-and-down year. More than one deal had fallen through but we also "caught a big one." I'd been the team lead on these deals representing my company to the other party. All through the year my boss and I had been connected through conversation, analysis of the deals, what was going right and what might have dropped through the proverbial crack. I felt day by day that I knew how he viewed the project and my contribution.

When it came time for a merit pay discussion, we had a rather brief phone call, similar in length to the one with my previous boss. There was a striking difference, however. He didn't have to describe the detailed pros and cons of my performance, although he had documented them on my review sheet, because he had communicated to me consistently throughout the year.

I received what I felt was a fair rating considering what the performance period had held, and above all, I knew where I had knocked it out of the park and where I could do better next time.

I hung up and felt like doing the Happy Dance.

This was the best of feedback because:

- Dialogue was continual and positive

- Specific (Detailed observations every step of the way)

- Two-way (I did mention dialogue, right?)

- Timely (Whenever the right and "real time" occurred—after the review, on the airplane, at dinner, in a meeting)

- Consistent throughout the performance period (I didn't have to wonder what he was thinking)

- Forward-looking ("Next time you might consider...")

Annual reviews sometimes get a bad rap and rightly so. One thing is certain: You don't want mentoring feedback, either as the giver or receiver, to be given in a way that feels rigid or perfunctory (or only happens once a year!) In a recent interview on National Public Radio (NPR), Samuel Culbert, management professor at UCLA, stressed, "Most people get worked up about [annual reviews] because, for employees, they don't like getting them and, for managers, they don't like giving them."[1]

Good or bad, your workplace is probably all about annual reviews. According to an October 2014 report from the Society of Human Resource Management, nearly 90 percent of companies do formal evaluations at least once a year.[2]

Recent statistics underscore the conclusion that individuals want more than an annual review and need steady, candid performance feedback.

- 50 percent of high performers expect at least a monthly sit down with managers to get feedback—only 53 percent of managers provide that.[3]

- 85 percent of Gen Y employees want "frequent and candid performance feedback" (only half of boomers agree)—interesting to note a generational shift that requires more frequent feedback.[4]

- Performance reviews are rarely or never "open, honest and meaningful" according to a majority (58 percent of U.S. and Canadian executives, managers and employees)[5]

Here's the good news for you about mentoring feedback...

Mentoring feedback is *not* an annual review.

Whatever your perceptions or experiences have been with what the NPR interview refers to as the "entrenched—and reviled—annual review,"[6] that does not apply to you in your mentoring relationship.

How to Both Give and Receive "Non-Annual Review" Feedback

So how do you give (and welcome) effective, timely, and useful feedback? Before we go any further, I want to stress the importance of frequent, informal conversations about how the mentee is progressing. Annual reviews often fail because so much time lapses between sessions and then they are awkward when they do occur. I call the feedback chapter in *MentorShift*, "Brief Debriefs" (p. 191) for a reason.

Make these conversations happen naturally and often.

Nowhere do I encourage a mentor to put on their coaching hat more than in the feedback arena. I offer a widely known coaching template, the "GROW" model[7], (not to be confused with our MentorShift, GROW, Step 3) attributed to Sir John Whitmore and his team of Performance Consultants, which embodies strong elements of a natural, conversant feedback process.

The "GROW" feedback model encourages questions. Mentor, your observations are important and your mentee's view of how they are doing is equally so. *By asking questions, you immediately establish that you want to have a discussion, not a monologue.* Then you interject truly positive observations and encouragements for the future as well.

The acrostic provides an easily accessible way to remember this feedback model:

G—GOAL—the endpoint where the mentee desires to be

R—REALITY—where the mentee is now

O—OBSTACLES and OPTIONS—whatever is stopping the mentee from getting where they want to go, and options to deal with those obstacles

W—WAY FORWARD—converting the obstacles into action steps that take the mentee to their goal

An example of a "Brief Debrief" using the GROW model appears below. The mentor offers feedback on how the mentee had led the meeting.

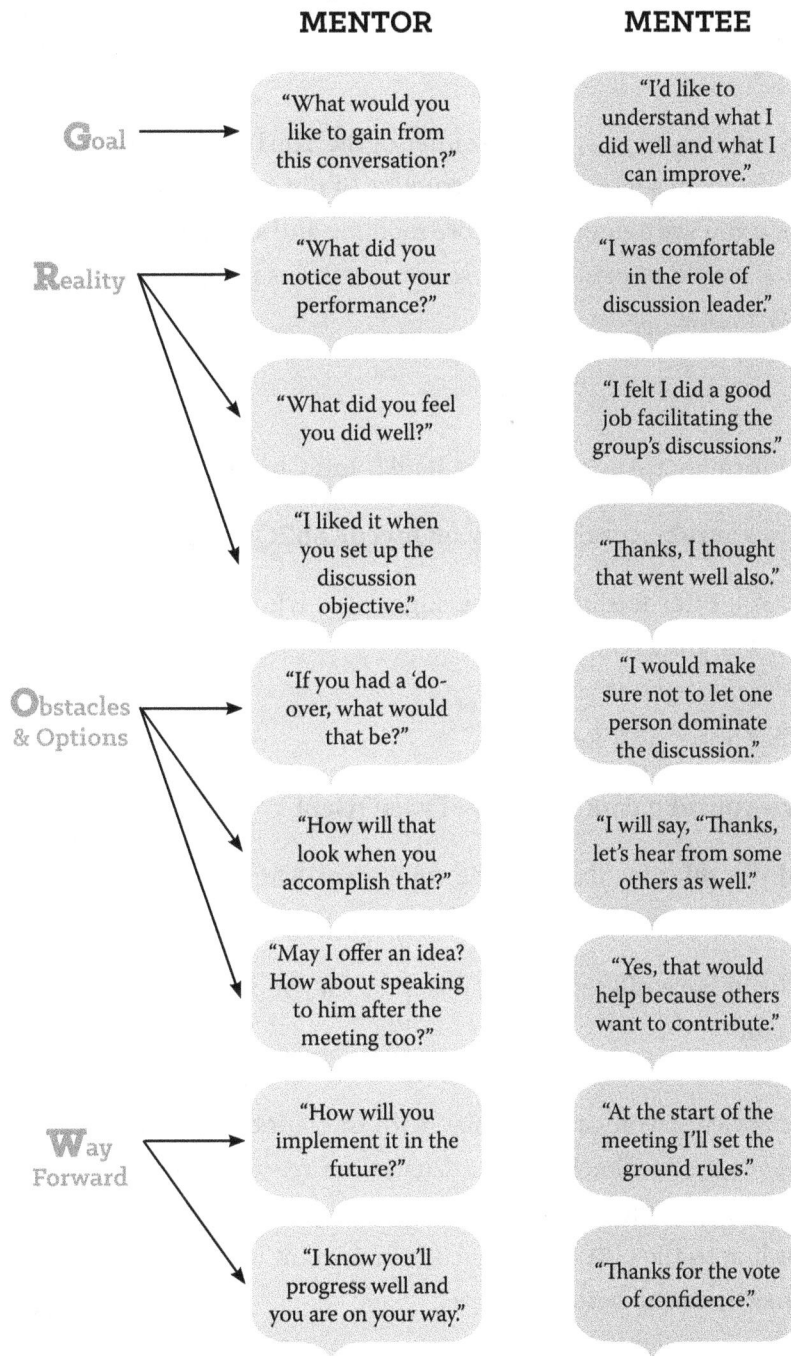

MENTOR   **MENTEE**

Goal

"What would you like to gain from this conversation?"

"I'd like to understand what I did well and what I can improve."

Reality

"What did you notice about your performance?"

"I was comfortable in the role of discussion leader."

"What did you feel you did well?"

"I felt I did a good job facilitating the group's discussions."

"I liked it when you set up the discussion objective."

"Thanks, I thought that went well also."

Obstacles & Options

"If you had a 'do-over, what would that be?"

"I would make sure not to let one person dominate the discussion."

"How will that look when you accomplish that?"

"I will say, "Thanks, let's hear from some others as well."

"May I offer an idea? How about speaking to him after the meeting too?"

"Yes, that would help because others want to contribute."

Way Forward

"How will you implement it in the future?"

"At the start of the meeting I'll set the ground rules."

"I know you'll progress well and you are on your way."

"Thanks for the vote of confidence."

Mentors, when offering feedback, asking questions and employing your version of the GROW model will optimize a positive conversation with your mentee.

Learning One Another's Feedback Styles

You now have a tool that you can use in a feedback discussion. It's helpful at this point to practice with the GROW feedback model and give yourselves an opportunity to learn each other's feedback styles.

To give you a bit of practice on this, choose either of the YouTube clips below. These clips show managers giving feedback in a less-than-constructive (if not humorous) way. View them when you are together or before meeting and share with one another how you would improve on these conversations using elements of the GROW model.

YouTube:

1. Google: "Performance Appraisal Gone Bad!!!" Joti Chana

   https://www.youtube.com/watch?v=eQbycpK8h7QGoogle

   How would you offer feedback to the supervisor who is giving his employee her annual review?

2. Google: Office Space TPS Reports

   https://www.youtube.com/watch?v=Fy3rjQGc6lA

   How would you offer feedback to the supervisor who clumsily gave coaching to the employee?

   How would you have offered the feedback to the employee for his minor error?

If you are an actor at heart, you can role-play with one another as to how you would deliver the feedback. If not, discuss the reasoning behind the feedback you would offer and most importantly, practice giving that feedback according to the GROW model. It's important to get in a rhythm of asking questions and being positive.

Betty By-the-Book-Mentor

"Here you go, straight from the classic tutorial, 'No Fuss Feedback.' Step 1: tell them what they did right. Step 2: tell them what they what they did wrong. Step 3: tell them to go work on it. Step 4: return to Step 1."

Offering Feedback for the Mentee's Pragmatics Project

Mentee, you've been working on your Pragmatics project for a while with your mentor. Use this opportunity to engage in a feedback conversation about how it's going.

Project: _____

_____

_____

Mentee

Prior to meeting with your mentor for a feedback conversation, write a few notes on the following questions.

1. What have you noticed about your performance?

_____

_____

_____

2. What do you feel you are doing well?

_____

_____

_____

3. If you had a "do-over," what would that be?

_____

_____

_____

Dan DevelopMentor

"Betty, giving feedback is an art. It's so important to make it a natural part of the mentoring process so it's not weird or awkward."

111

4. How would you implement it in the future?

_____

_____

_____

Mentor

Prior to meeting with your mentee for a feedback conversation, take a few notes on the following questions.

1. Look back at page 103, the GROW model conversation. What questions will you ask your mentee?

_____

_____

_____

_____

2. What have you liked about your mentee's performance? What do you suggest that your mentee improve or strengthen?

_____

_____

_____

_____

Betty By-the-Book-Mentor

"A natural part of the mentoring process? Is that Step 5?"

3. On what positive note will you conclude your feedback time?

_____

_____

_____

4. What can you do to help them improve?

_____

_____

_____

MODULE 7	SHIFT MATRIX (Example) The Power of Good Feedback	
Pragmatics Project: To lead a major contract negotiation		
	Mentor	**Mentee**
S Share • Mentor: Share what you feel the mentee did well • Mentee: Share what you feel you did well	• *I felt my mentee handled the prep well, she had done our company's research thoroughly* • *My mentee can grow in analysis of competitive position*	• *I did a good job of pulling together relevant points that would strengthen our position. I could have spent more time analyzing the other side's points to prepare for rebuttal*
H How • Discuss how your assessments of what the mentee did well are in agreement and how they are different.	• *I think we both felt my mentee had prepared well for our side and that improvement on anticipating their arguments needs to be improved*	• *I think we both thought I'd done my homework and prepared us well for our point* • *My mentor feels quite strongly that I need much more time preparing rebuttals; I thought I did fairly well so I need to understand that viewpoint*
I Insight • If there was a "do-over" what would that be and what would it look like?	• *Mentee might consider reviewing the prior negotiation meeting notes and shoring up rebuttals based off that.*	• *I would make sure I was better equipped with the other side's current position, where they were weak and how we could capitalize on our strong points.*
F Focus in Focus in (ending the discussion positively) • Mentee: What was the most valuable thing you learned while doing your Pragmatics task? • Mentor: What talent or skill did you observe in your mentee that you hadn't seen before?	• *Mentee has a lot to bring to the negotiation table. Answers questions in a straightforward manner and is clear in explanations.*	• *I learned that being sharp on the points of our side is not enough; I need to anticipate the other side's arguments and motivations as well. That will heighten my chance for negotiation success.*
T Task/Time • When will mentee complete these improvements? When and where will the mentor and mentee meet to work on them?	• *In our next negotiation round coming up in two weeks. We need to meet next week to shore up our competitive arguments.*	• *I start tomorrow to prep for next round of negotiations. I'll meet with my mentor next Monday to work on the other side's position*

Key Step 3 (Feedback) Thought:
• Mentor—When you hold a feedback discussion, ask questions!

MODULE 7	SHIFT MATRIX The Power of Good Feedback	
Pragmatics Project:		
	Mentor	**Mentee**
S Share • Mentor: Share what you feel the mentee did well • Mentee: Share what you feel you did well		
H How • Discuss how your assessments of what the mentee did well are in agreement and how they are different.		
I Insight • If there was a "do-over" what would that be and what would it look like?		
F Focus in Focus in (ending the discussion positively) • Mentee: What was the most valuable thing you learned while doing your Pragmatics task? • Mentor: What talent or skill did you observe in your mentee that you hadn't seen before?		
T Task/Time • When will mentee complete these improvements? When and where will the mentor and mentee meet to work on them?		

Key Step 3 (Feedback) Thought:
• Mentor—When you hold a feedback discussion, ask questions!

Summary and Next Steps

Feedback is an essential part of any mentoring relationship. It is not an "annual review" format, but rather a continual dialogue with support as the mentor converses with the mentee on strengths and room for "do-overs." Good feedback propels the mentee to grow and gain confidence.

In Module 8, you will look together toward the mentee taking full responsibility for the project and the mentor assuming a supportive role on an as-needed basis.

Step 4: GO "You Do"

Go Forward with a Successful Launch

"Go back?" he thought. "No good at all! Go sideways? Impossible!
Go forward? Only thing to do! On we go!"

J.R.R. Tolkien, *The Hobbit*

When should you end your mentoring relationships and launch your mentees out on their own? Great question. It can happen too soon, too late or at just the right time. Listen in on a few "launching" conversations conducted by our mentoring friends, Dayna Drive-By, Harry HoverMentor, and Adam AchieveMentor.

Three "Out to Launch" Conversations

Launched Too Soon—"Where Did She Go?"

MENTEE: "I'm looking forward to talking some more about my GROW project. I'd like to hear what your thoughts are about how I handled my part of the negotiation."

DAYNA: "I think you were superlative! You're ready to go! Please do call if you have any questions about future negotiations. If I'm in town I'll be happy to connect with you."

MENTEE: "Really? I was thinking we need to do some debriefing about it and then we could do the bigger negotiation together next week.

DAYNA: "Heavens, no! You rocked it when you presented our case. I think it's better if I cut you loose right here and now. Good luck my friend, it's all good from here on out!"

Dayna Drive-ByMentor

Launched Too Late—"We're Meeting Again?"

HARRY: "I'm so glad you made it for our meeting. I wanted to take some time right off the bat to plan our next few meetings. There's a never-ending list of opportunities to develop you! I think we should plan on a bi-weekly meeting through the end of the year, agree?

MENTEE: "Well, I was thinking we could probably just check in casually from time to time from now on. We finished my Pragmatics Project last month."

HARRY: "Oh, we'd be missing the accountability. And I think we can fine-tune your learning on that project just a bit more."

MENTEE: "We did say we'd end our formal meetings at the end of six months."

Harry HoverMentor

HARRY: "Oh, nonsense! What were we thinking? We're just getting started! Okay, let's get our calendars out!

Launched at The Right Time—"All Set to Go?" "Yep, Fire the Ignition!"

ADAM: "Like I shared in our earlier debrief, I really see growth in how you are handling the tough questions in negotiations and responding in the moment. Are you feeling pretty good about what you've achieved?"

MENTEE: "I think I've come a long way. I know we said we'd meet for six months and we're there now. This seems like a perfect time for me to pick up the future negotiations on my own."

ADAM: "I think you're ready too. I'm always around for a phone call if you want to run some strategy ideas by me. I won't disappear off the face of the earth."

Adam AchieveMentor

MENTEE: "That's great, thanks. I will call if I need to and then let's plan to meet in a few months for a drink or better yet, a chance for me to beat you again in a one-on-one game of hoops!"

ADAM: I'll take that challenge on anytime! I don't know about who will beat who but that all sounds great... and good luck!

What a difference in these conversations! It's not hard to see which one ended well. I know you want a positive ending for your mentoring relationship too, so let's make sure you have a winning finish.

What's the Optimum Way to End the Mentoring Relationship?

In Module 4, you established the mutually desired timeframe for your mentoring relationship. You chose that timeframe up front so you could ensure that you have:

- Accountability throughout the course of the relationship

- Check-in times and an agreed upon exit point

- No "weirdness" or awkwardness for either party at the end

If you designed the relationship to be nine months, for example, the mentor needs to be evaluating if the mentee is ready to launch by that time and the mentee needs to be considering that question too. If the mentee is not ready to launch, discuss if it's reasonable to extend the relationship and how much time will be needed.

Is the Mentee Ready for Launch?

How will you know?

Mentor, have you given your mentee the amount of time and attention they needed to move on? More than 37 percent of the graduate students in mentoring relationships at the University of Northern Colorado said in a recent survey that the top way to improve their experience would be to have more time with their mentors.[1] So when you assess your mentee's readiness, be sure to ask if they've had enough time with you to reach their goals.

The mentee's progress and confidence on their Pragmatics Project should give you and your mentee a good sense of whether they're ready to be launched.

Mentor and Mentee—to prepare for completing the MentorShift matrix together, answer these questions individually before you meet.

1. Has the Mentee successfully demonstrated proficiency in their Pragmatics project? If so, how? If not, why not?

    _____

    _____

    _____

2. How has the mentee implemented the mentor's feedback and suggestions for improvement?

    _____

    _____

    _____

3. What sort of feedback did the mentee get from other people who observed their projects or presentations?

4. How confident do you each feel about the mentee's ability to consistently perform the proficiency well, without the support of the mentor?

5. Has the mentee achieved the goals for the mentoring relationship to their satisfaction and to the mentor's?

6. Is there any unfinished business that you need to wrap up together?

What Does Good Closure Looks Like?

My mentees have shared a couple of stories with me about less-than-positive endings to former mentoring relationships. Here is the essence of a couple of those real-life conversations.

"The Prolonged Parting"

ME: "Mateo, how is mentoring going for you and Tyson?"

MATEO: "Who knows? I thought we were supposed to be finished last month, at least that is what we'd originally planned. He keeps moving out our meetings on the calendar and then we generally don't even have them. I'm not sure if we're finished or not.

A couple of months later...

ME: "How did things wind up with Tyson? Are you two still meeting together?"

MATEO: "Well, sort of. We had coffee last month but then he is on a big project for the next few months so he said he'd get back with me. It's odd, though, because we said we'd be finished a few months ago and yet we're not. He still calls to check in once in awhile. I'm not sure why we haven't moved on. I guess I should be the one to say something."

Need I say more? The Prolonged Parting.

"The Abrupt Adios"

ME: Anya, how are things going with Gina?

ANYA: "I haven't heard from her in two months."

ME: "Weren't you planning to meet twice a month?"

ANYA: "We had been meeting that often. Then we just stopped. I'm not sure if we're off or on. I should probably ask her but it is just awkward. I see her in the hall and I'm not sure if I'm supposed to just say 'hello' and keep going or ask about our next meeting."

Once again, The Abrupt Adios.

Neither the Prolonged Parting nor the Abrupt Adios is any way to conclude your mentoring relationship. You can see the dilemma from the conversations above,

- One or both are uncertain as to the state or progress of the relationship

- Interactions can be awkward and uncomfortable

- Frustration, particularly on the mentee's part

In a CBS news report, *Mentoring Tips*, Deborah Radman, then senior vice president/director at CKPR television station, says, "Scheduling a formal ending is an important event in the mentoring relationship, a time when you can celebrate your accomplishments and plan for the future. A formal ending prevents the relationship from dwindling without focus or disintegrating from inactivity."[2]

It also gives each mentoring partner *a needed sense of closure* and a transition into a less formal partnership or a new mentoring arrangement. It's an excellent time to evaluate your work together, finish your last objectives, and plan for future options."

After all the good work you've done together, don't let the ending be the Prolonged Parting or the Abrupt Adios! Rather let it be:

- Intentional, timely and planned

- Mutually agreed upon

- After you've achieved the goals the mentee set out to accomplish

You started this mentoring relationship to support the mentee in achieving specific goals, including a measurable improvement in a proficiency demonstrated by the mentee's Pragmatic Project. Once the mentee has achieved their goals and is ready to move forward on their own, it's time for the mentor to take on a new mentee and time for the mentee to become a mentor. But not so fast. Here are a few final ideas to make launch worth remembering:

Ask yourself:

- How will we track, report and celebrate results so we hold ourselves accountable for progress?"

- How can you, the mentee, demonstrate that you know and that you've grown?

  - Will you do a task independently?

  - Will you take over leadership of the task?

- How can we set up ongoing progress?

- How can we share the measurable, tangible results?

  - You've finished your project, so share your outcomes with your stakeholders – perhaps a new process, an updated system, a white paper, reduced cost

- Celebrate the good work together!

  - You've been committed and worked hard—how about a drink, dinner, cup of coffee, or at least a high five?

- Verbal or written acknowledgements to one another

  - Send an email or write a quick note to the other person to acknowledge the time and effort they've put in and why you benefited from the time together. It never hurts to say "Thanks!"

- What do we look like now? (Final launch or return to earth?)

  - Clearly agree on the "going forward."

    - Do you call it quits and that's it? (Nothing wrong with that, good job)

    - Do you plan for a regular, occasional meet-up to check in?

    - Do you make it casual? ("Swing by if you have any issues you ever want to talk over.")

    - Whatever you do, make it CLEAR.

The Shift Matrix below will be your last official task together ,unless you've chosen to extend the mentoring relationship for a designated amount of time.

MODULE 8	Step 4—"GO" Go Forward with a Successful Launch

Pragmatics Project: To lead a major contract negotiation		
	Mentor	**Mentee**
S Share • Mentor and mentee: Share why you believe the mentee is ready to be launched.	• *My mentee has demonstrated in three different negotiations readiness to handle the preparation and conduct of a negotiation.*	• *I've conducted three negotiations and have taken all elements of the last one—the prep, facilitation, management debriefs and finalization of the deal.*
H How • Share how confident you feel about the mentee performing their new skills without support from the mentor.	• *Mentee is very competent and will likely only need help on an occasional basis.*	• *I feel confident to perform mid-size to large negotiations.*
I* Insight • What would be a visual and/or tangible proof of result that could demonstrate the success of this project and your mentoring relationship?	• *I'm very satisfied that mentee is ready to go out and accomplish the same tasks without me in the picture very much. Able to handle all elements of a negotiation.*	• *Specifically, I've learned to control my responses to an irate "other party" and to guide the discussion in a more positive manner. My mentor demonstrated that cool-headedness when I observed her early on.* • *I'm satisfied with what I've learned because conducting a negotiation effectively was my main goal. I'm ready to lead the next major negotiation.*
F Focus in • Mentor and mentee: Discuss any unfinished business that you agree is important to wrap up prior to ending the mentoring relationship.	• *I just want my mentee to know that they can call if needed to check in at anytime. I have a vested interest in their success!*	• *I would like to arrange to a meeting or phone call once a quarter, just to stay sharp on new strategies and approaches.*
T Task/Time • When will the mentoring relationship officially end?	• *Officially? Next month.*	• *It will end after our next meeting.*

*Key Step 4 Thought: At this point, you'll both want measurable proof that the mentee's pragmatic project is successful and thus the mentoring relationship has been value-added.

MODULE 8	Step 4—"GO" Go Forward with a Successful Launch	
Pragmatics Project:		
	Mentor	**Mentee**
S Share • Mentor and mentee: Share why you believe the mentee is ready to be launched.		
H How • Share how confident you feel about the mentee performing their new skills without support from the mentor.		
I* Insight • What would be a visual and/or tangible proof of result that could demonstrate the success of this project and your mentoring relationship?		
F Focus in • Mentor and mentee: Discuss any unfinished business that you agree is important to wrap up prior to ending the mentoring relationship.		
T Task/Time • When will the mentoring relationship officially end?		

*Key Step 4 Thought: At this point, you'll both want measurable proof that the mentee's pragmatic project is successful and thus the mentoring relationship has been value-added.

MentorShift Roadmap
Four Step Process

Go
"Results–Track–Celebrate"

_____
_____
_____
_____

Grow
"Challenge/Growth Areas"

_____
_____
_____
_____

Show
"With Experiences"

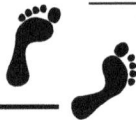

_____
_____
_____
_____

Know
"Project Definition"

_____
_____
_____
_____

GO Example:*

My mentor has invited me to stop by occasionally to share any status or issues. We will go forward informally with no set future meetings planned.

*When moving to the GO phase and thus a different phase in your relationship, be sure expectations are clear for both mentor and mentee.

NOTE: Refer to Appendix, Module 8, for additional blank sample of Four Step Process Roadmap

Summary and What's Next

Congratulations to both of you. When the mentee is ready to launch, it's a job well done by mentor and mentee.

So it seems the mentoring is all wrapped up.

Well, not quite yet.

KNOW.... SHOW.... GROW.... GO

Mentoring That Multiplies

The Never-Ending Circle of
KNOW. SHOW. GROW. GO.

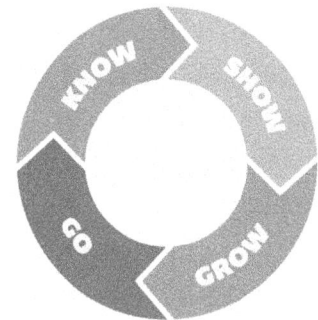

"The wheel is come full circle."

William Shakespeare

Whether you are 18 or 88, you've likely come across the imaginative and heart-warming play or movie, *The Lion King*. After following the tempestuous journey of the lead character, Simba, from cubhood throughout his trials, travails, and passions, and into his own coming of age, you witness him at the story's end as he stands triumphantly atop Pride Rock, a beaming father, and nobly presents his own baby cub, Kiara, for the world to admire and embrace. What is he doing?

Of course: He is celebrating the Circle of Life.

People possess a strong and motivating force to bring something or someone into existence, further that growth and development, and live to see that person or idea do the same. Mentoring creates a type of parenthood, if you will, for all who endeavor to do it well. It's a certain way to multiply and keep the beat going on.

In this final module, you will be encouraged to think about your own circle of life, not in the existential or philosophical sense, but in the forward-looking, practical sense as it relates to your own mentoring relationships. You will examine how to make it happen, but first, a view as to the phenomenon of multiplying mentors and what multiplying mentors (and as a counterpoint, "non-multiplying mentors") look like.

Paying it Forward—Are Multiplying Mentors a Fact of Life or a One-in-a-Million Phenomenon?

This circle of "paying it forward" weaves throughout the fabric of our everyday lives. It's an old concept, possibly coined in early 20th-century literature. It's been used in legalese to describe paying a debt forward by lending it to a third person rather than paying it back to the original lender. More recently it's been popularized in the movie, "Pay it Forward," where a young boy does three good deeds for others in need and in return, asks is that they pass on the good deed to three other people and keep the cycle going. In 2014, 70 companies participated in "Pay it Forward Day!"[1] Many would argue it's in our DNA to want to take what we've gained personally and multiply it for the good of others.

So, are mentors in business actually paying it forward, or better said for our purposes, "mentoring forward"?

Talent research firm, Catalyst, conducted a study of alumni who had attended MBA programs at 26 leading business schools throughout the world. Based on responses from 742 respondents who had attended full-time MBA programs and had worked full-time at a company or firm, they found that the men and women who were more likely to be developing others:

- Had themselves received developmental support (59 percent) vs. those who have not received this type of support (47 percent)

- Were sponsored (66 percent) as opposed to not receiving sponsorship (42 percent)

The study concludes, "High potential talent who were themselves mentored, coached or sponsored to advance in their careers are more likely to 'pay it forward' by developing the next generations of leaders."[2]

You might be wondering, "Is there more benefit than just the human 'feel good' part of mentoring forward?" In fact, there is. In a financially encouraging side note, the study reveals, "Paying it forward pays back: It benefits not only protégés but leads to career advancement and compensation growth for those providing the assistance—$25,075 in additional compensation between 2008 and 2010, according to the report." It goes on to say, "Why? It might be that developing other talent creates more visibility and following within the organization for the high-potentials who are doing the developing, which leads to greater reward and recognition for the extra effort."[3]

According to this study, mentoring forward is a fact of life (although I would submit not as much as it could and should be) and occurs even more for those who have themselves been mentored well.

Preparing to Become a Multiplying Mentor

You and your mentee have decided it's time for launch, but you don't want to end there. The following questions will stimulate thinking as to how you will "move forward to mentor forward." Both mentor and mentee will want to think through these, as you both move forward to mentor again.

Mentor

1. List three skills or talents that you strengthened in yourself during the mentoring relationship.

2. How did being in this mentoring relationship benefit you professionally and/or personally?

3. What, if anything, will you do differently in your next mentoring relationship?

4. What did you teach or show your mentee that will make a positive difference for them in their career?

_____

_____

5. What suggestions would you give your mentee about being a good mentor?

_____

_____

6. List three people who can benefit in the future by learning what you are most inspired to share?

_____

_____

Mentee

1. List three skills or talents that you strengthened during the mentoring relationship.

_____

_____

2. How did being in this mentoring relationship benefit you professionally and/or personally?

_____

_____

3. What, if anything, will you do differently in your next mentoring relationship?

_____

_____

4. What did you learn or observe that will make a positive difference for you in your career?

_____

_____

_____

5. What suggestions would you give your mentor to help them grow?

_____

_____

_____

6. List three people who can benefit by learning what you are most inspired to share.

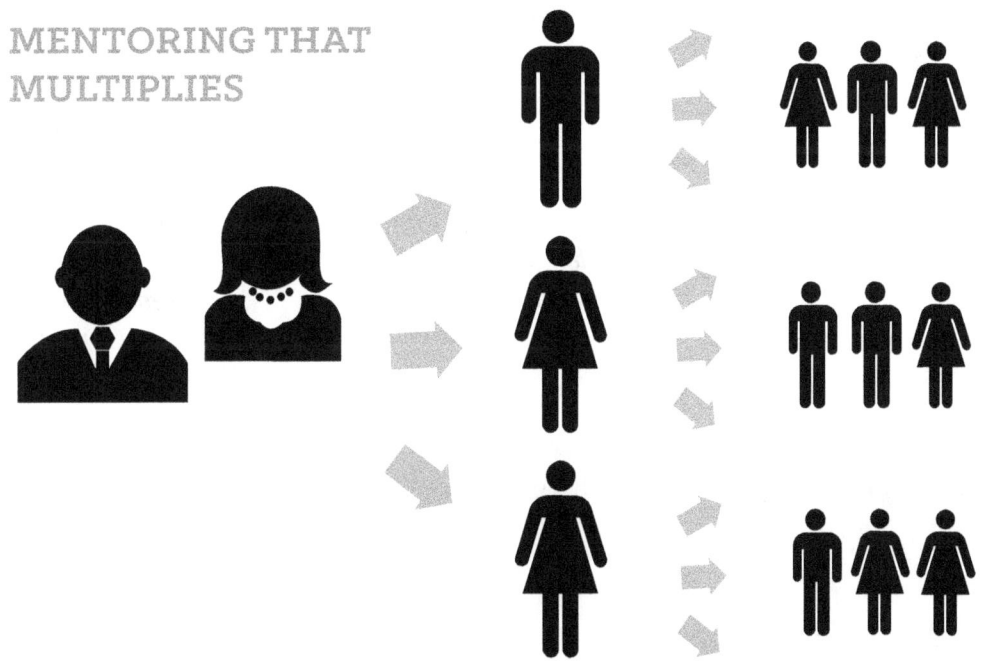

_____

_____

_____

MENTORING THAT
MULTIPLIES

MODULE 9	SHIFT MATRIX (Example) Mentoring that Multiplies	
	Mentor	**Mentee**
S Share • Why do you feel it's an important step to "mentor forward?"	• *I know I'm grooming others and transferring knowledge that is important for our company.*	• *I've learned a lot from going through the MentorShift process with my mentor. I want to share it with someone else while the experience is still fresh in my mind.*

H How
 • How will you identify your next mentee?
 • Who comes to mind as you consider this?
	• *Several individuals have expressed interest in a mentoring relationship. I will likely talk with a couple of them to check availability.*
	   • *John Doe*
	   • *Sally Smith*
	   • *Ashley Jones*
		• *I will talk with my boss about potential mentees. Also ask a couple of my friends for individuals they'd recommend.*
		   • *Rob Johnson*
		   • *Sarah White*
		   • *Bill Black*

I Insight • What is the downside of not mentoring forward? • What are the benefits for you personally? To your organization?	• *Downside is limited knowledge transfer* • *Others not developed* • *Benefits to me—knowledge that I'm investing in the future and "giving back"*	• *Downside is I would have experienced this good relationship and let it stop there. No one else would benefit.* • *Benefits to me would be that I would be investing in someone who needs some help and I would be perceived by mgmt. as a team player*
F Focus in • How specifically will you approach/ask your next mentee to join you in a mentoring relationship? • How can you apply principles from the MentorView?	• *I will ask one of the three I mentioned above for a cup of coffee to talk about it.* • *I can listen to what they are looking for specifically and share what I'd like to offer.*	• *I will ask my mentor now to meet up with my potential mentee and me and we'll talk about what a relationship could look like*
T Task/Time • When will you reach out to your next mentee?	• *By end of the month*	• *I will do it this week*

MODULE 9	SHIFT MATRIX Mentoring that Multiplies	
	Mentor	**Mentee**
S **Share** • Why do you feel it's an important step to "mentor forward?"		
H **How** • How will you identify your next mentee? • Who comes to mind as you consider this?		
I **Insight** • What is the downside of not mentoring forward? • What are the benefits for you personally? To your organization?		
F **Focus in** • How specifically will you approach/ask your next mentee to join you in a mentoring relationship? • How can you apply principles from the MentorView?		
T **Task/Time** • When will you reach out to your next mentee?		

Summary and Next Steps

As you are ending your trip through this MentorShift supplement, I'd like to encourage you that "You can do this!" Look what you've done together over the past months. I'd also suggest that when planning a new mentoring relationship, you can make it a win/win proposition by having the mentor and mentee meet with the new potential mentee to describe the process they've just completed. It offers a helpful view to a mentee-to-be to see the success and power of the MentorShift process and hear your personal testimony. Give it a try!

Concluding Note to Readers

"To succeed in life you need two things;
ignorance and confidence."

Mark Twain

When I began writing both the MentorShift book and now its supplement, friends would ask me, "What will be your measure of success?" To me, that translated as, "How will you know that the process you preach is doing one darn bit of good to anyone?"

"Fair question," I would routinely answer, openly acknowledging their astounding insight for posing such a probing question. And then I would immerse myself in any activity to which I could inconspicuously escape. Quietly, I would retreat to do some belly button pondering in search of the deep, existential answers they ... and maybe I ... were looking for. How *would* I know that the MentorShift process that I trust and believe in was doing anyone any good at all?

I found that I could only ponder my belly button for so long. And besides, like most truths, the answer was simple, and was there all along.

I resonate with Mark Twain's witticisms and particularly with the opening quote above. When it comes to a mentoring process and all of its intricacies, obstacles, challenge and rewards, I know that I am both ignorant and confident.

There is much I don't know about mentoring (and life for that matter). There are situations that might arise in my own mentoring endeavors to which I might not know the answer. The process that I rely on might not have the immediate solution at times. But I've been at the MentorShift process for enough years—and seen enough lives changed—that I do know enough to be boldly, brashly and wholeheartedly confident that it will carry you and me from a beginning, never-before mentee to a strong and capable multiplying mentor.

This would be my measure of success—that you would not stop at reading a book about mentoring or filling in blanks in a workbook, but rather that you would invest in at least one other person in this lifetime and show them how to mentor as well.

See, I said it was simple.

So, good luck to you. I know you can do it, and you've worked hard to learn a process that you can always carry with you.

A Parting Conversation Among "The Mentors"

ADAM ACHIEVEMENTOR: So team...how do you think it went? Do you think the readers are ready to mentor forward with the MentorShift process?

AUGIE ARGUMENTOR: I'd argue that they need some more training. One pass through a workbook is not enough. In my studies I've found that in order to cement in a habit, a person has to practice it 34 times. So let's create 33 more possibilities for these learners.

EMMA ENJOYMENTOR: Augie, I've said it before and I'll say it again, you need to chill, my friend! Let them have some fun and don't put them through the ringer with 33 more workbooks!

BETTY BYTHEBOOKMENTOR: They can accomplish what they need if they just follow this workbook. And of course they could fill out some more forms, long ones. And keep a daily mentoring journal. That keeps a strict discipline so they don't veer off the path. Wouldn't that be fun, Emma?

EMMA ENJOYMENTOR: I think your definition of fun is a little different than mine, Betty.

BETTY BYTHEBOOKMENTOR: You say "fun"? Saturday night in the library is a great night for me!

DAN DEVELOPMENTOR: Let's get back on track. The readers will create their own style with the process and everyone moves forward at their own pace. That's the way it should be.

HARRY HOVERMENTOR: If the readers need any assistance with their mentors or mentees I can join them in every meeting—just to keep a presence, you know. And then of course, debrief afterwards. And then call them that evening at home for Q and A.

CARRIE COMMITMENTOR: Um, Harry, I think that would be a bit much. You want to keep in touch based on what they need and want, right?

HARRY HOVERMENTOR: Well, I would think they would need and want my help!

DAYNA DRIVEBYMENTOR: Hey you two, I hate to interrupt. I just thought I'd drop in and add my two bits. Oops. My two bits will have to wait though, since I'm off to my next meeting. Back soon!

CARRIE COMMITMENTOR: Anyway, I think it's been a fruitful journey for the learners and I trust they'll keep on mentoring and being mentored. Everybody agree?

ADAM ACHIEVEMENTOR: I'd say we're all on board with that, except for Dayna. Does anybody here know where she is?

DAN DEVELOPMENTOR: I don't know, she was here a minute ago....

Appendix

Module 4—Step 1: KNOW. The Five Powerful Proficiencies

- Finding your strengths

  - StrengthFinder 2.0

- Multiple Intelligences Test

  http://www.literacynet.org/mi/assessment/findyourstrengths.html

- Workunu Strengths Test

  http://freestrengthstest.workuno.com/free-strengths-test.html

- VIA Institute on Character Assessment

  http://www.viacharacter.org/www/

- The Standout Assessment

  http://www.tmbc.com/store/standout-assessment

Module 8 The four step form

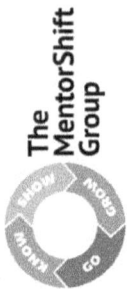

MentorShift® 1-1 Project

Mentor _____   Mentee _____

☐ KNOW/Project Definition

☐ SHOW/Planned "With" Activities

☐ GROW/Specific Desired Mentee Growth Area(s)

☐ GO/Tangible Evidence of Project Progress or Completion

The MentorShift Group

144

About the Author

Lori Bachman is the Founder and CEO of The MentorShift Group.

After a rewarding financial career in the aerospace industry, Lori moved into a second career as an advocate for the importance of mentoring. Through The MentorShift Group, Lori and her team help corporations, associations, government agencies, and non-profits tap into, expand, and leverage their talent pool.

Through her instructive, inspiring four-step MentorShift process, she guides individuals to greater personal and professional development and leads businesses to improved performance, productivity, and profits. Her book, *MentorShift*, and now the companion supplement, *MentorShft at Work*, underscore the philosophy and practice she shares with businesses on a mentoring mission.

Lori is an internationally respected business consultant, author, keynote speaker, and training workshop leader. Her audiences and clients include:

- Amgen

- Lockheed Martin

- First Data

- Gates Corporation

- Vectra Bank

- Brocade Communications

- Nelnet

- Great-West Financial

- Square Two Financial

David B. Morgan, Senior Vice President, Morgan Stanley shares, "I've seen Lori in action. She's a walking, talking role model of why mentoring is important. I am so glad she is dedicating herself to showing organizations how they can raise their morale and improve their workplace culture by instituting effective mentoring practices."

Would you like to prevent brain drain and leverage the talent in your organization? Contact us if you would like to:

- Honor your employees
- Experience expertise and insights by giving them practical ways to pass what they've learned to others
- Connect team members through a proven process that gives them an opportunity to make a difference for all involved
- Codify workplace knowledge so it can be replicated by others

Lori's services are available via:

- Full complement of workshops
- Corporate and association keynotes
- Conference breakout sessions
- Internal training programs
- Customized consulting

We look forward to hearing from you! You can reach her at **www.loribachman.com** or **lori@loribachman.com**. Here's to great mentoring!

Endnotes

Module 1

1 Jacques, R. (2013). 16 wildly successful people who overcame huge obstacles to get there. *Huffpost Healthy Living*. Retrieved from http://www.huffingtonpost.com/ 2013/09/25/successful-people-obstacles_n_3964459.html

2 *Touch the Top*. Erik Weihenmayer. (2015). Retrieved from http://www.touchthetop.com

3 Alcorn, R. (2010). Florence Chadwick and the fog. *Eternal Perspective Ministries*. Retrieved from http://www.epm.org/resources/2010/Jan/21/florence-chadwick-and-fog/

4 Sinek, S. (2009). How great leaders inspire action. TED. Video. Retrieved from http://www.ted.com/talks/ simon_sinek_how_great_leaders_inspire_action?

Module 2

1 Washington, D. (2011). The mentors he'll never forget. *Guideposts*. Retrieved from http://www.guide-posts.org/inspirational-stories/inspiring-story-denzel-washington-finds-success-help-mentors

2 Kahle-Piasecki, L. (2011). Making a mentoring relationship work: What is required for organizational success. *Journal of Applied Business and Economics* 12(1), 51. Retrieved from http://www.na-businesspress.com/jabe/piaseckiweb.pdf

3 Bova, M. (n.d.). Code 400 orientation for flight programs and project directorate: "Mentoring for success." *Marilou Bova*, Inc., 6 & 17. Retrieved from fpd.gsfc.nasa.gov/ code400_orientation_ session.doc

4 Kahle-Piasecki, 51.

5 Kahle-Piasecki, 51.

6 St-John, E., & Audet, J. (2009). Factors leading to satisfaction in a mentoring scheme for novice entrepreneurs. *International Journal of Evidence Based Coaching and Mentoring* 7(1), 148-161. Retrieved from http://web.b.ebscohost.com.ezproxy2. library.colostate.edu: 2048/ehost/pdfviewer/ pdfviewer?sid=32a0cb54-5de7-414e-963d-da124f263a1c%40sessionmgr198&vid=11&hid=125

7 Leonard-Wilkinson, T. A. (2003). The mentor advantage. *Intercom 50*(4), 36 & 41. Retrieved from http://web.b.ebscohost.com.ezproxy2.library.colostate.edu: 2048/ehost/pdfviewer/ pdfviewer?sid=32a0cb54-5de7-414e-963d-da124f263a1c%40sessionmgr198&vid= 19&hid=125

8 Leonard-Wilkinson, 2003, 36 & 41.

9 Leonard-Wilkinson, 2003, 36 & 41.

10 Leonard-Wilkinson, 2003, 36 & 41.

11 Sandberg, J. (2008). With bad mentors, it's better to break up than make up. *Wall Street Journal*, Eastern edition. New York, New York. Retrieved from http://search.proquest.com.ezproxy2.library.colostate. edu:2048/docview/399091148?accountid=10223

12 St-John & Audet, 2009, 148-161.

13 Marbella, J. (2012). Bob Bowman has proven to be more than Michael Phelps' coach. *The Baltimore Sun*. Retrieved from http://articles.baltimoresun.com/2012-07-25/sports/bs-sp-olympics-bow-man-20120725_1_bowman-and-phelps-bob-bowman-hilary-and-whitney

14 Wescott, D. (2013). Mentorships: A selection from history. *Bloomberg Business*. Retrieved from http://www.businessweek.com/articles/2013-03-14/mentorships-a-selection-from-history

15 Wescott, 2013.

16 Wescott, 2013.

Module 3

1 *The New York Times.* Bolt blamed in shuttle's failure at tethered flight. (1992). Retrieved from http://www.nytimes.com/1992/08/30/us/bolt-blamed-in-shuttle-s-failure-at-tethered-flight.html

2 Morris, B. (2006). New rule: Look out, not in. Old rule: Be lean and mean. *Fortune.* Retrieved from http://archive.fortune.com/2006/07/10/magazines/fortune/ rule4.fortune/index.htm

3 *Six Sigma.* What is six sigma? (n.d.) Retrieved from http://www.isixsigma.com/ new-to-six-sigma/getting-started/what-six-sigma/

4 *Six Sigma*, n.d.

5 *iSixSigma.* Six Sigma. (2015). Retrieved from sixsigmanonline.org

6 *Six Sigma*, n.d.

Module 5

1 *Chicago Tonight*, "Becoming a Man — Promising Sports Program Cuts Violent Crime Arrests for Students," July 16, 2012, Retrieved from http://chicagotonight.wttw.com/2012/07/16/becoming-man

2 Youth Guidance, (2012). BAM — Sports Edition [Video] Retrieved from https://www.youtube.com/watch?v=18wq9v1n9n0

3 *Youth Guidance: Guiding Kids to Bright Futures*, (2016), Retrieved from https://www.youth-guidance.org/bam/

4 *Youth Guidance: Guiding Kids to Bright Futures*, (2016)

5 Youth Guidance, (2012). BAM — Sports Edition [Video]

6 Wake Forest Baptist Medical Center (2013). Neuroscientists explain how the sensation of brain freeze works. *ScienceDaily.* Retrieved from http://www.sciencedaily.com/releases/2013/05/130522095335.htm

7 *Fact Slides.* Brain facts: 36 facts about the brain. (n.d.) Retrieved from http://www.factslides.com/s-Brain#

8   Society for Neuroscience (2012). Are you born with all your brain cells, or do you grow new ones? *Brain-Facts.org*. Retrieved from http://www.brainfacts.org/about-neuroscience/ask-an-expert/articles/2012/are-you-born-with-all-your-brain-cells-or-do-you-grow-new-ones

9   Schank, Roger C. (1995) What We Learn When We Learn by Doing. (Technical Report No. 60). Northwestern University, Institute for Learning Sciences.

Module 6

1   Edwards, D. (2014). American schools are training kids for a world that doesn't exist. *Wired*. Retrieved from http://www.wired.com/2014/10/on-learning-by-doing/

Module 7

1   "Behold the Entrenched—and Reviled—Annual Review." *Morning Edition*. National Public Radio (NPR). KCFR, Denver, October 30, 2014. Radio.

2   "Behold the Entrenched—and Reviled—Annual Review."

3   Willyerd, K. (2014). What high performers want at work. *Harvard Business Review*. Retrieved from https://hbr.org/2014/11/what-high-performers-want-at-work

4   Hite, B. (2008). Employers rethink how they give feedback. *The Wall Street Journal*. Retrieved from http://online.wsj.com/articles/SB122385967800027549

5   Berman-Gorvine, M. (2014). Performance reviews get negative rating from most execs and employees. *Bloomberg BNA*. Retrieved from http://www.bna.com/performance-reviews-negative-n17179911165/

6   "Behold the Entrenched—and Reviled—Annual Review."

7   Haughey, D. (2014). Better coaching using the GROW model. *Projectsmart.co.uk*. Retrieved from http://www.projectsmart.co.uk/better-coaching-using-the-grow-model.php

Module 8

1   Black. L. L., Rizzolo, S., & Knippenberg, S. (2012). Exit survey: Spring 2012 and summer 2012. *University of Northern Colorado: Graduate School and International Admissions*. Retrieved from http://www.unco.edu/grad/about/pdf/ Summary%20report%20Spring%20and%20summer%202012_Exit%20Survey.pdf

2   Radman, Deborah. (2009, March 18) Mentoring Tips. *CBS News*. Retrieved from http://www.cbsnews.com/news/deborah-radman-mentoring-tips/

Module 9

1   *Pay It Forward Day*. (2015). Retrieved from http://payitforwardday.com

2   *Catalyst*. (n.d.) Paying it forward pays back for business leaders. Retrieved from http://www.catalyst.org/media/paying-it-forward-pays-back-business-leaders

3   *Catalyst*, n.d.